WHEN ELEPHANTS FIGHT

Adrian and Jimmy catch up, talking family, football and the future.

When Elephants Fight

The lives of children in conflict in afghanistan, bosnia, sri lanka, sudan and uganda

Eric Walters & Adrian Bradbury

ORCA BOOK PUBLISHERS

This book is dedicated to those most innocent
victims of war: children.
—EW

For Isaac and Owen. You are why I am changed
and why today, I remain the same.
—AB

Library and Archives Canada Cataloguing in Publication

Walters, Eric, 1957-
When elephants fight / written by Eric Walters and Adrian Bradbury.

ISBN 978-1-55143-900-6 (bound).--ISBN 978-1-55469-355-9 (pbk.)

1. Children and war. I. Bradbury, Adrian, 1970- II. Title.
HQ784.W3W35 2008   305.23086'949   C2008-903027-3

First published in the United States, 2008
Library of Congress Control Number: 2008928576

Summary: The lives of children in conflict in Afghanistan, Bosnia, Sri Lanka, Sudan and Uganda. Portaits of five child victims of conflict, including regional history, maps and the causes and results of the conflict.

Orca Book Publishers gratefully acknowledges the support for its publishing programs provided by the following agencies: the Government of Canada through the Canada Book Fund and the Canada Council for the Arts, and the Province of British Columbia through the BC Arts Council and the Book Publishing Tax Credit.

Cover photo and all photos in the Uganda section courtesy of Colin O'Connor.
Photos from *My Childhood Under Fire: A Sarajevo Diary* written by Nadja Halilbegovich used by permission of Kids Can Press Ltd., Toronto; photos © Halilbegovich and Morrison families.
Kim Phuc photo courtesy of Kim Phuc.
Photos on pages 37, 41, 50 and 55 © Getty Images; photos on pages 33 and 67 © Dreamstime.com.
All other photos courtesy of GuluWalk.

Cover design and interior maps by Allen Ford
Interior design by Teresa Bubela

ORCA BOOK PUBLISHERS
PO Box 5626, STN. B
VICTORIA, BC CANADA
V8R 6S4

ORCA BOOK PUBLISHERS
PO Box 468
CUSTER, WA USA
98240-0468

www.orcabook.com
Printed and bound in Hong Kong.

13 12 11 10 • 4 3 2 1

CONTENTS

Bosnia

The Sudan

FOREWORD

by Kim Phuc

There can be no doubt that in any war the most innocent, those who have had no part in the creation of the conflict, are the children. It is equally clear that there has been no war fought in which children were not those who suffered the most. Unable to flee, unable to defend themselves, unable to even understand, they have been the ones who have felt the effects of war the most. I know this because I was one of those children.

I grew up in Vietnam at a time when the country had been at war much longer than I had even been alive. The violence and conflict were always a part of our lives, even in the times of complete calm and quiet. You tried to live a normal life—going to school, working the fields, playing with your friends, eating with your family—but knew that life could instantly be altered or ended. You could only hope and pray that you and your family would be spared.

For me that veneer of normalcy was shattered forever when I was nine years old. Our village was at the center of a pitched battle. As we were seeking shelter from the fighting, we were accidentally hit with a type of bomb that contained napalm— chemicals that cause things to break into flames. My clothes, and then my body, caught fire. All I remember clearly is the pain. Over 65 percent of my body was burned, and I was supposed to die. I was hospitalized for fourteen months, undergoing seventeen surgical procedures and extensive and painful therapy and rehabilitation before finally leaving the hospital behind.

My plight, my personal tragedy, was captured by photographer Nick Ut. This picture, which won the Pulitzer Prize, became a visual image of the horror of war and the effects on the most innocent, children.

When Elephants Fight is dedicated to allowing the reader to look into the eyes of five children who have experienced war and to hear their personal stories. Jimmy, Nadja, Annu, Farooq and Toma have lived through the trauma and tragedy of war. Their stories are taken from five different places around the world—Uganda, Bosnia, Sri Lanka, Afghanistan and the Sudan. They are all different, but they are the same in that they are the stories of individual children. War affects millions of people, but each of those people is an individual, and the most vulnerable are the children.

Along with the personal accounts of these children, the authors have provided the background to these five conflicts—the history of the country and the conflict—that led to the unfortunate circumstances that altered the lives of the children. By understanding what causes conflict, we are better equipped to understand how future conflicts may be avoided.

It is human nature to want to turn away from tragedy, but we must remember the words of Dr. Martin Luther King, who said, "Darkness cannot drive out darkness; only light can do that." I ask you not to look away. Look into the eyes of these five children—hear their stories and appreciate that these children could be your children, could be you. Let in the light.

I still bear the scars of what happened to me. I still feel the physical pain daily. The past remains part of me. I feel it is important not to pretend that terrible things don't take place. We should not forget, but we must also learn to forgive, and take an active role in helping those who have suffered and try to ease their pain.

With love,
Kim Phuc

KIM FOUNDATION INTERNATIONAL
healing children of war

Kim Phuc Bio

Kim was born and raised in Trang Bang, a small community north of Saigon, during the Vietnam war. In 1972, at the age of nine, while fleeing for safety, she and others were mistakenly bombed with napalm by a South Vietnamese airplane.

Kim remained in Vietnam after the fall of the country to communism. As adults she and her husband defected in 1992, taking refuge in Canada. In 1994 she became a goodwill ambassador for UNESCO, traveling the world to speak out about the terrible effects of war on children and the need for peace, love and forgiveness.

She founded the Kim Foundation, whose mission "is to help heal the wounds suffered by innocent children and to restore hope and happiness to their lives by providing much-needed medical and psychological assistance." Her foundation funds projects around the world.

Kim resides in Ajax, Ontario, Canada, with her husband and two children, Thomas and Stephen. She is a living symbol of the strength of the human spirit to overcome tragedy and is a shining example of the power of love, forgiveness and reconciliation.

For further information visit: www.kimfoundation.com

For a more detailed look at Kim's life and the impact of the famous photograph, see *The Girl in the Picture: The Story of Kim Phuc, Whose Image Altered the Course of the Vietnam War*, by Denise Chong and published by Penguin.

INTRODUCTION

When elephants fight, it is the grass that suffers.

T his saying is an ancient proverb of the Kikuyu people, a tribal group in Kenya, Africa. While the source of this quote is lost in the distant past, the wisdom is as true today as when those words were first spoken, perhaps thousands of years ago. Its essence is simplicity. When the large—the strong, the dominant— fight, it is the small—the weak, the least powerful—who suffer most. Regardless of which elephant wins, or loses, the grass beneath their feet will always be trampled and destroyed.

Joseph Stalin, former Soviet leader, stated, "The death of a million is a statistic, the death of one, a tragedy." We will start with the one.

When Elephants Fight tells the story of five children, one from each of five very distinct conflicts around the world—Afghanistan, Bosnia, the Sudan, Sri Lanka and Uganda. We hope that these five stories will demonstrate the devastating impact that war can have on young inno- cent bystanders. Through these very personal accounts we hope you will not only feel the pain these children have suffered, but also both sympa- thize and empathize with them. After all, but for the accident of birth, this could be you. Along with each eyewitness account, we have tried to briefly present something of the history and geopolitical background of the conflicts in each country.

There has never been a war fought that was started by children—or one that failed to harm them. Children are the grass beneath the feet of the men, the tribes, the armies and the nations engaged in armed conflict. Regardless of the winner—and there is a strong case to be made that war produces no winners, only greater and lesser losers—the children always suffer.

Although it might be argued that in some wars efforts are made to spare children, this is, in fact, an

4

impossible task. Children must *always* suffer the consequences of armed struggle. The fact of the matter is that we live in a world with limited resources and these resources cannot be used for both the purposes of war and the provisions of peace. Every act of war steals resources that could be used to build schools and hospitals, plant fields and feed the hungry.

In every war there is always collateral damage. This is the politically correct term that describes a situation in which an intended target is missed and something— or someone—else bears the brunt of an attack. A military position is targeted, but the school or church or mosque next to it is destroyed by artillery fire, bombs or missiles. A bullet is aimed at a soldier but hits a woman or child hiding in the ditch behind him. Military experts assert that no war is possible without collateral damage—it is inevitable, and by being inevitable, somehow it becomes acceptable. Strangely, this term involves both property and people, as if one is no more important than the other.

Collateral damage can involve the destruction of a hospital, a school, an orchard or a crop. The damages done to these properties might ultimately cause the death of more people than the battle itself. A school is destroyed, and future doctors and engineers and teachers are never trained. A hospital is destroyed, and the sick die and diseases spread. A field, crop or well is destroyed, and malnutrition, deprivation and starvation take lives. In almost every war ever fought, there were more lives lost because of the effects of the war than those lost on the battlefield. Starvation and disease ultimately kill and maim more people than those claimed by direct conflict.

In some conflicts children are not collateral damage, not a sad secondary effect of war, but the *specific* targets of war. They are seen as equally valid targets of death as any armed combatant. Perhaps, by some sick and twisted logic, they are even seen as *better* targets than an armed combatant. They can't fight back.

In the greatest of human atrocities, armed combatants actively seek out any member of a group in an attempt to eradicate, eliminate and annihilate that group. We are, of course, talking about genocide. Genocide by definition is the deliberate and systematic destruction of a group based on race, religion or culture.

The genocide most known to the modern Western world is the Holocaust that took place in Europe from 1939–1945, when Nazi Germany attempted to eliminate all Jewish people and certain other ethnic minorities. This atrocity resulted in millions of men, women and children being systematically identified, captured, transported and slaughtered.

It would be tempting to view the Holocaust as just a temporary insanity that involved one group of people. This is not the case. Within the last one hundred years alone, genocide has taken place in Armenia, Cambodia, Rwanda, Yugoslavia, Russia, the Sudan and China. It would be an underestimation to say that over one hundred million people were killed in these periods of genocidal insanity. And each of those victims, regardless of the specific conflict, was equally human and equally important, and the loss of life equally tragic.

There are times when children are not even targeted because of any ethnic, racial or religious reason, but simply because they are children. They are the most vulnerable as well as the most impressionable targets. They are removed by armed men from the safety of their homes and the care of their families so that they can be used as servants, slaves or sexual partners, or they are forced to become combatants in the conflict.

The legacy of child soldiers is one of the greatest tragedies of this past century. Young children are taken from their families by armed combatants. Family members are slaughtered—sometimes children are forced to take the lives of members of their own families. Young children, some younger than ten years old, become indoctrinated and trained in the ways of killing. They become efficient killers for the same reason that children can become such agents for good—they are impressionable, open and too young to understand the ultimate consequences of their actions.

One of the first steps in training for armed combat is to dehumanize, minimize and distance those being targeted from those who will do the killing. This may seem a somewhat unlikely proposition from our vantage point in the Western world. Nevertheless, we know it happens. Although we might be geographically and politically distanced from the war zones of today's world, we must never assume that we are somehow superior to people who find themselves in the midst of these conflicts.

Some readers will almost certainly claim that *When Elephants Fight* presents a biased view of the stories presented. Despite our best efforts to present the full picture, this is an inevitable reality. These criticisms will be founded not so much on the validity of our efforts as on the personal passions that these conflicts arouse. And, equally certain, since we view our world through the eyes of our own personal history, some of this criticism will be valid. We acknowledge that we enter this project with a clear and stated bias. This bias is best put into words by former United States president and humanitarian, Jimmy Carter: "War may sometimes be a necessary evil. But no matter how necessary, it is always an evil, never a good. We will not learn how to live together in peace by killing each other's children."

Children around the world suffer from the consequences of war. We live in a time and place where our children have escaped not only the direct consequences of these wars but even the *knowledge* of these conflicts.

For the future to be better than the past, better than the present, we must help equip our children with the awareness and understanding of the world around them and their ability to bring about change. Gandhi stated, "If you are going to change the world, start with the children."

With the purchase of this book you have helped children who have suffered from war—royalties from this book are being donated to GuluWalk to help children affected by the war in Uganda. For more information visit www.guluwalk.com.

When
Elephants
Fight

— Afghanistan
— Uganda
— Sri Lanka
— Sudan
— Bosnia and Herzegovina

JIMMY

Walking Away from Danger

"It is time!"

Startled out of his thoughts, Jimmy looked up at his grandmother standing on the edge of the field, waving.

"It is time!" she yelled again, not sure she'd been heard or seen.

Jimmy waved back to acknowledge her. He looked up at the sun. He could tell from its position in the sky, starting to sink toward the trees, that she was right. It was time to go. Jimmy's brothers, Christopher, Julius and Douglas, working away in the field beside him, had heard her as well. They nodded their heads in agreement. Jimmy swung the hoe over his shoulder. For Douglas, only six and small for his age, the hoe was as big as he was, and it weighed heavily on his shoulders. Maybe Jimmy could have helped but he knew his littlest brother had to learn to bear his share of the load. There was no choice.

As they walked through the field, Jimmy thought about their crop.

The field was planted in root vegetables, mainly cassava, with only the tops showing through the soil so far, but it looked like there was going to be a good harvest. He prayed for a good harvest. Without that there'd be more times when hunger would be with them.

Today the four brothers had finished weeding four rows. He knew that Christopher, the oldest at fourteen, had hoped for more, but there wasn't time. There was never enough time.

By the time they reached their home—two small huts, with the charred remains of a third beside them—their grandmother was waiting. One hut belonged to the boys. The second hut was their grandmother's. The third used to be their uncle's home.

Grandmother had packed them a small cloth bag. Inside was a little bit of food. Not much, but enough to give them something to eat on the road,

Jimmy poses next to the prints of his mother's hands on the wall of the room where he now sleeps.

and, if they rationed it out, perhaps a bite for the morning before they set out again. Christopher would carry the food and decide when they would eat. Jimmy didn't know when he would choose to let them eat something, but he did know it would be done fairly, each receiving his share. Maybe there wasn't enough, but whatever they did have was shared equally. That had always been the way in his family.

Jimmy also wanted to take one more thing with him. He ran into the hut and found it right where he'd set it down—on the little wooden stool that his father had made.

It was a book with dog-eared corners, the cover partially ripped and the pages soiled from so many students having used it over the years. But it was important that he bring it along. There was a test tomorrow, and he'd already missed a day of school this week to sell vegetables by the roadside. He knew that he needed to study. Hopefully there would still be enough light to see the book when they arrived.

It would be so much easier if they could just stay on their land. There would be more time to work in the fields. Time to study. Time to sleep. But not tonight. In fact, not any night for as long as Jimmy could remember. It seemed like forever since he'd been able to sleep in his own house.

There was a time, more than a year ago, when each evening his grandmother and older brother would make a decision—was it safe to stay or did they have to go? While they were at school or working in the fields, Grandmother would listen to the radio, or talk to neighbors or relatives, people who lived in the village, and find out if there had been any attacks in the area. Some nights there was no word; nothing had happened. Then they might risk staying. But it was always a risk. There were no guarantees. Jimmy knew that better than almost anybody.

It had been quiet that night when the Lord's Resistance Army had come to his village. The rebel soldiers ordered everybody out of the huts and made them all kneel on the hard-packed earth of the yard and—he didn't want to think about it anymore. There wasn't even time for memories or grief. There was just time to walk. It was almost comforting to realize that there was no decision to make. Now, every night was too dangerous to stay.

Grandmother gave each boy a hug. As Jimmy wrapped his arms around her, he felt nothing but bones. She wasn't well and she didn't eat enough to get better. Whatever scraps of food that were left were meant for her grandsons. Each evening, as he said his good-byes to her, he wondered if he would see her when he returned in the morning. He wished that she could come with them, but he knew she was too old and too sick to make the trip.

Besides, the soldiers left old women alone. She wasn't strong enough to work or young enough to bear children. She wasn't somebody they could make into a soldier, or somebody that they had to fear. She was just an old woman, a grandmother, and she was of no use to them. Not even worth the price of a bullet. But he still worried. There was no cost in the blow of a machete.

Some of these people—and Jimmy hardly even saw them as people—didn't need a reason to kill. Maybe they were high on drugs or simply lusted for blood and didn't need a reason. He could only hope that they didn't want to even waste the energy necessary to strike her down. They left old women alone…they left old women alone…that's what he'd heard. That was the thought that kept his hopes alive. They didn't bother with old women.

He had to hope that's how she was seen: a worthless old woman. But to Jimmy and his brothers, she was all they had. If something happened to her, who would cook their meals for them? Who would help work the fields or bring water? Who would Christopher talk to when he needed to make decisions? Jimmy knew his brother was smart and he trusted him, but still, he was yet to turn fourteen. He still needed the advice of his grandmother.

"We have to go," Christopher said softly.

Without another word they started off. It was a long walk, but the first steps were always the same and provided them with a vivid reminder of why it was they needed to walk. There were three mounds behind the huts, just off the path they took. Jimmy cast only a sideways glance as they passed—maybe it wasn't respectful—but he just didn't want to look, couldn't dwell on what had happened and how much he missed them. Too many memories.

Jimmy envied his littlest brother. He was only two at the time and was too young to remember it. All he knew were the stories that he'd been told. Jimmy would never forget, never get those images out of his mind.

As the boys walked they were joined by other children leaving their families behind. There was already a trickle of other kids on the dirt track. As they passed each new home, each cluster of houses, each village, they were joined by more and more children. Some of these children were relatives and some were friends. None were strangers. Walking together each night and back again in the morning left little time for the fields or for schoolwork, but lots of time for talking. It was almost ironic that during these long walks, with nothing else that could be done, the children were free to be children. They sang songs, or played games, talked and laughed as they walked. They tried to make the best of it. But what choice did they have? To stay in their homes in the isolated villages and countryside was to risk being killed or kidnapped. So each night they walked, leaving their homes behind, heading for the safety of the town of Gulu, where they could be supervised by relief agency staff and guarded by government soldiers.

The children moved to the side of the road as two vehicles rumbled up behind them. One was a van driven by one of the relief agencies, and the second was a big army truck. As the second truck passed, he saw the soldiers, rifles in hand, sitting in the back. Even they didn't want to be in the country or on the roads when darkness fell. And, if it was even too dangerous for them, how much more dangerous was it for the children being left behind on the road as dusk rapidly approached?

Jimmy looked behind him. As far as he could see there were children walking. Looking forward the line stretched out of sight as well. Next he looked on both sides of the road. Huts dotted the hills; small stalls—roadside stores—were frequent. Everything seemed as it should be. They were safe. At least for now. At least until darkness fell. He found himself quickening his pace.

In some ways Jimmy and his brothers were lucky. For them the walk was only six or seven kilometers. They could make the trip in less than two hours. He knew of other children who were traveling twice as far.

Then there were those who were too far away to make the walk. Rather than seeking a blanket in the town, they simply left their homes, left their villages and headed into the forest. Some would dig shallow depressions in the ground, lie down and push dirt back over themselves like a blanket to provide protection from the elements, animals and any prying eyes. Others hid in thickets, while some built crude shelters in the branches of trees. Jimmy couldn't imagine having to live like that, sleep like that every night, but for them, as with his family, what was the choice?

Everybody in the whole Gulu district knew what might happen to those who stayed behind. Jimmy had met people who had been attacked, hands or feet hacked off by blows from a machete or their lips and ears sliced off with a razor. He'd never forget the first time he'd seen somebody who had suffered that fate. Then there were those who were taken. Young girls were kidnapped to be sex slaves and young boys were taken at gunpoint to become child soldiers, leaving behind murdered parents and looted and burned villages.

As darkness started to settle in, Jimmy felt that sense of uneasiness that he always felt at night. Still, he was reassured by what he could see ahead—the glow of lights in the sky marking the town of Gulu. And, on the road all around him were more and more children. Each little trickle, each stream, coming from all directions, had become a human river, and they were moving along in the current.

The houses and stores became more frequent as they approached the town. And those buildings became more solid, made of brick and stone and blocks, some two- or even three-stories tall. Lights glowed from upper-story windows or storefronts. Around them, standing at watch, clustered together in little groups, sitting in trucks or vehicles, were soldiers and police. Strange: they fled men with guns to come here to be protected by other men with guns.

Some of those stores remained open just for the night commuters, those who had a few shillings to purchase food. Here, every night was crowded like a market day. The streets were filled with thousands of people, mostly children, although they weren't here to buy or sell, but simply to find a place to lie down for the night, to sleep.

Most of the children had a place that they sought out, that they were familiar with. For Jimmy and his brothers it was a hostel called Noah's Ark. It was run by UNICEF—United Nations International Children's Emergency Fund. The staff who ran the shelter were friendly and treated the children well. Each night the boys registered, were given a blanket to use and went to find a piece of ground where they could spend the night. In the space around them were other children. Jimmy didn't know how many, but most nights there were between three and four *thousand* children. And that was just a percentage of the night commuters. Throughout the town there were half a dozen places, run by other aid agencies, church groups and the government. And even with all of those places, there were still those who simply slept on the streets. At least they were safe. And what choice did they have?

Jimmy took his blanket, laid it down on the ground and wrapped

REPUBLIC OF UGANDA

Population: 27,600,000

Location: Latitude: 3° 13' 60 N, Longitude: 31° 52' 0 E, east Africa

Area: 236,040 square kilometers

Climate: tropical, equatorial climate

Languages: English (Official language) 74%
Swahili (Official language)
* over 30 languages used in Uganda (predominantly Bantu and Nilotic languages)

Ethnicity: Buganda 16%
Iteso 8%
Basoga 8%
Banyankore 8%
Banyaruanda 6%
Bakiga 7%
Lango 6%
Bagisu 5%
Acholi 4.5%
Other 31.5%
* over 30 ethnic groups in Uganda

Religion: Christian 85%
Muslim 12%
Other 3%

Life Expectancy: 52 years

Infant Mortality Rate: 66 deaths per 1,000 live births

Per Capita Income: $1,100

Literacy rate: 66.8% (male: 76.8%, female: 57.7%)

Children at Pagak Internally Displaced Persons (IDP) camp.

himself in it to ward away the night chill. Douglas placed his blanket down next to Jimmy, followed by Julius and Christopher on the far side so the two oldest sheltered the two youngest.

All around them the other children were settling in for the night. Some of the younger children had already gone to sleep; others sitting on their blankets and talking; while some were off to the side, talking or playing simple games. Jimmy didn't have time for games. He needed to study. He took the book and angled it so that he could catch a little bit of light from the bulb that hung overhead in the corner. It was dim and far away, but there was enough light for at least a few minutes to study before it was turned off for the night.

Christopher opened the little sack that their grandmother had prepared for them. He took out the two pieces of bread that it held, divided them in two and shared them between the four boys. This would have to hold them, through the night and the walk back to their home. Their grandmother would be waiting with a little more breakfast for them, some cassava, maybe some more millet. The boys would do a few chores, and then they would walk to school. After school they would go home, help to gather water, work the fields and get ready, once again, to walk to Gulu. Night after night, day after day, that was the life Jimmy knew. Each day going to school, or working the fields, doing chores, selling vegetables at the side of the road. Each evening walking to Gulu. Each night sleeping at Noah's Ark. And each morning walking back home. It had been going on for years. It was the only life the younger children even knew. But Jimmy remembered a different time, a time before they had to seek shelter in the town every night, before the deaths. Sometimes he just wished he could forget that night when everything changed. It had now been four years, but in some ways it seemed like it had just happened.

It was a quiet night. They'd gone to sleep, the four boys, Christopher 10, Jimmy 8, Julius 6 and Douglas just 2. They nestled together in one room, on the right side of the hut, with their parents in another room to the left. It was a comfortable home, cream-colored clay walls, a tin roof and door and a dirt floor. Across the way their uncle, their father's younger brother, slept in his hut, and in the third, their grandmother.

Jimmy was awakened by screaming and yelling. There was pounding on the door, and then the door was kicked open.

They were hauled out, half sleeping, half in shock, crying, powerless beneath powerful flashlights, and forced to drop to their knees in the dirt, their hands on the back of their heads. His parents and uncle were knocked to the ground, their hands tied behind their backs. And all the time the men screamed out threats, saying they would kill them all if anybody resisted

The men—no they weren't all men, some were barely boys—stood over them, waving guns, yelling, screaming. Some were dressed in uniforms, others in nothing more than pants and heavy jackets. All wore gumboots. On the ground, not daring to look up, partially blinded by the lights shining in their faces, all Jimmy could see were the boots.

The men—the boys—walked down the line, screaming, yelling, threatening to harm or kill as they passed. Jimmy knew these weren't just idle threats. And now he was on the ground, kneeling at the feet of the people who committed these atrocities, and all he could see were their boots.

Under the glare of the bright lights, surrounded by darkness, his parents bound, screams and threats raining down on them, Jimmy knew that these could be the last moments of his life, or at the very least, the life he knew.

Suddenly his parents and uncle were grabbed and hauled to their feet, dragged away. The last words his father screamed were "please, I beg you, don't

Jimmy taking a break in the tree that provides shade for the family home.

hurt our children!" and then they disappeared into the night, swallowed by the darkness.

Almost before the words had faded, the boys were grabbed and hauled to their feet. They were dragged back to their hut and thrown through the door, landing in a heap on top of each other on the dirt floor. The door was slammed shut, and all four huddled together as the men screamed outside. They heard objects being thrown against the door to barricade them in. Were they being left...or were they trapped inside, barricaded, unable to leave before the hut was set on fire?

Christopher tried to quiet the tears of Julius and Douglas. Jimmy listened at the door, straining to hear anything...but there was nothing. Silently they stayed in the hut, still afraid to cry out, afraid to even try to break through the door and escape. What if the men were still close by? What if they heard and came back to get them...to kill them?

Jimmy wasn't sure how long they stayed in the hut. He wasn't sure if he had drifted off to sleep, but he did know what happened next. Finally Christopher felt that enough time had passed that it was safe for them to try to get out.

They pounded at the door, they called out and they were heard—by their grandmother. She was old and hard of hearing and had slept in her hut, unaware of what had happened. She pulled away the barricade and opened the door, and the four boys almost toppled her over as they rushed out.

The soldiers of the Lord's Resistance Army were gone. And with them were Jimmy's parents and uncle, leaving the old woman and the four children behind—the children who were too young to become soldiers. At least too young that night.

When morning finally broke, their grandmother went in search of her two sons and her daughter-in-law. Where had they been taken? Where were they? She started to ask questions and to search, but she didn't have to look long or far. They were discovered in a field less than a kilometer away. The bodies of the three were found beaten, hands still bound behind their backs, with a bullet in their skulls. They'd been dragged away simply to be killed.

The neighbors helped bring back the bodies, helped dig the graves and helped put the bodies to rest. And they were there, in those mounds just off the path, within sight of the homes where they had lived their lives.

Since then it was just the four boys and their grandmother. Their parents were dead, but the people who killed them were still around, still killing and kidnapping. It wasn't safe for the boys to remain in their home at night, but they still needed to return each day to work the fields to grow food to live, to go to school and to have any hope for a better future. So each night and each morning, they walked to and from Gulu, seeking shelter and safety. Constantly in motion, never having time to rest or stop. But what choice did they have?

Follow-up: Jimmy

Jimmy is now seventeen years old and still lives in the three-room family home near Gulu, with his three brothers and his ailing grandmother. His impeccable English has been featured in a segment of the documentary film *Uganda Rising*. He now ventures into town daily to attend computer classes, and he hopes to return to school full-time early next year.

UGANDA

History

The Republic of Uganda is located in eastern Africa. It is a landlocked country that sits directly on the equator and is bordered on the west by the Democratic Republic of the Congo, on the north by Sudan, on the east by Kenya, on the south by Tanzania and on the southwest by Rwanda. While not a coastal country, Uganda is surrounded by an abundance of water, including Lake Victoria to the south, Lake Albert to the west and is cut down the middle by the Nile River.

Winston Churchill, former prime minister of the United Kingdom, once praised Uganda's beauty by saying, "For magnificence, for variety of form and color, for profusion of brilliant life—bird, insect, reptile, beast—for vast scale—Uganda is truly the pearl of Africa."

Uganda's history began about two thousand years ago when it was first populated by the ironworking Bantu-speaking people of central and western Africa. They were joined from the north by the Nilotic people, including the Luo, whose lifestyle centered around cattle-herding and farming in the northern and eastern parts of what is now Uganda.

The first external influence in the region came from Arab traders moving inland from the Indian Ocean in the 1830s. They came in search of slaves and ivory. They were closely followed in the 1860s by the British who were exploring the source of the Nile River.

In the late 1880s the United Kingdom put the area under the charter of the British East Africa Company, which became part of the colonial "scramble for Africa" in which European nations staked their claims on African resources and its people, for their own gain. The region was initially a collection of kingdoms led by chiefs and clan leaders. These groups were changed forever by this influence from outside, but the different groups still are at the core of who Ugandans are today.

In 1894, Uganda was ruled as a protectorate, and the Bantu-speaking people of the south were placed in civil service positions, while the Luo of the north, mainly the Lango and the Acholi, were forced into labor camps and the military. This divided the nation in two classes, increasing the tension between the groups. This divide would be most evident after independence and is, to a great degree, responsible for the seemingly endless military coups and rebel uprisings that have plagued the nation.

The first of those military coups came from the notorious Idi Amin. In 1962, less than nine years after independence, Amin ousted Uganda's first president, Milton Obote. Amin was responsible for the death of as many as 300,000 Ugandans, while also expelling the Indian community, who controlled a major stake in the country's economy. Originally seen locally and internationally as a welcomed change, Amin's rule of bloodshed and shortsightedness sent the country into a downward spiral. Inflation climbed to 1000% and unpaid soldiers rebelled. Amin finally sealed his own fate by choosing to go to war with Tanzania.

The Tanzanians took control of Uganda and turned on the local population, who they claimed to be helping, while Amin fled to Libya. Obote's reinstallation as president in 1980 was short-lived, as was Tito Okello's military coup. In 1986 Yoweri Museveni took power when his National Resistance Army (NRA) claimed the capital.

Museveni quickly introduced economic reforms that provided some sustained growth in Uganda and he was lauded as a "new breed of African leader," by then United States president, Bill Clinton. What continued to be ignored was Uganda's north-south divide, which proved to be the birthplace of the worst of rebel uprisings.

The Conflict

The ongoing civil strife in northern Uganda is a conflict that continues to be misunderstood. The war is essentially two conflicts in one: first, the fighting of the Lord's Resistance Army (LRA), which is waging war against the Ugandan government and terrorizing the civilian population in the north, and second, the real grievances of Ugandans in the north against the existing government.

The war arose out of the embedded policy of the British during colonial rule in which tribal groups were divided. This 'divide and rule' policy was continued by post-colonial Ugandan politics. When the current president, Yoweri Museveni, and his National Resistance Movement took power

A view south into Gulu, northern Uganda's largest town.

by coup in 1986, they worsened the north-south divide by alienating northerners, creating grounds for rebellion.

Since 1986, the insurgency within northern Uganda has undergone four stages, beginning with a more popular rebellion of former army officials and evolving into the current pseudo-spiritual warlordism of the LRA. To date, the LRA consists mainly of abducted children brainwashed, brutalized and forced to kill viciously as child soldiers. Alienated from the Acholi, the LRA wages terror on the civilian population as a means to maintain attention and challenge the government.

After attempted peace talks facilitated by Betty Bigombe collapsed in 1994, the conflict changed into a proxy war that cannot be understood separate from the geopolitics of the entire Great Lakes Region of Africa.

In 1994, the country of Sudan began to provide military assistance and support to the LRA, while the Ugandan government provided military assistance to the Sudan People's Liberation Army (SPLA), a rebel group in southern Sudan. The West, particularly the United States, saw this as the battlefront of the war against the spread of Islamic fundamentalism in sub-Saharan Africa and provided significant amounts of aid to the SPLA through Uganda. New elements of a war economy and arms trafficking made finding peace more difficult.

Following September 11, 2001, the United States increased its strategic alliance with President Museveni and his NRM regime in Uganda. The U.S. quickly declared the LRA a terrorist group and increased military aid to the Ugandan government. This relationship only further solidified the insistence of Museveni on a military approach to end the war. Unfortunately, the "military solution" has worsened northern grievances and proven ineffective over the years. It is strongly believed that rather than continued war, that the keys to peace are to negotiate and build mutual trust.

In the summer of 2006, the newly formed semi-autonomous Government of South Sudan agreed to host and mediate peace talks between the warring parties. The involvement of such a strategic mediator, coupled with new openness by the parties to negotiations led many to call this the "best opportunity in over a decade for peace in northern Uganda." In August, the parties agreed to a Cessation of Hostilities—to stop fighting—that led to relative calm in northern Uganda. However, the talks have since stumbled due to the rigid involvement of the International Criminal Court (ICC), a weak Monitoring Team and divisions within the LRA networks.

The war in northern Uganda has raged now for 21 years, making it Africa's longest-running conflict,

and has been described by one UN official as "the world's worst neglected humanitarian crisis." The war has led to the displacement of 1.7 million people—over 80% of the region—who now live in camps in squalid conditions. At its worst, 1,000 people were dying each week as a result of the poor conditions in these camps. The war is also known for the brutal abduction and use of child soldiers. The LRA has filled its ranks by abducting over 50,000 children.

As this neglect continues, the people of northern Uganda remain condemned to lives of despair and displacement.

Child Soldiers

For over 250,000 children all over the world, army barracks are home and military commanders are family. These are no ordinary children. They are child soldiers.

There is still no universally accepted definition for what a child soldier is, but international human rights organizations, including UNICEF, agree that a child soldier is a boy or girl under the age of eighteen who willingly joins or is forced to become a member of a government army or rebel-armed military. These child soldiers are commanded to perform a variety of duties, including armed combat, laying mines and explosives, scouting, cooking and labor, and are often victims of sexual slavery and exploitation.

Today, children are directly participating in conflicts in over 20 countries worldwide, with more than 100,000 children on the frontlines in Africa; most prominently in Sudan and Uganda, where it is estimated that the Lord's Resistance Army has abducted 50,000 children and forced them into conflict.

While thousands of children are indeed abducted or recruited by force, many more join voluntarily. However, they often enlist as a means of survival: joining because of extreme poverty, lack of education or family support, along with the promise of a steady income, status and power, which most often never comes. The military is seen as their only opportunity to get ahead during a time of unbelievable desperation. The majority of child soldiers are between the ages of 14 to 18, but there are children as young as 9 years of age who have been forced into conflict.

For those not familiar with the child soldier phenomenon, it's difficult to understand the value of an army of young children. When we hear the word "soldier" we automatically think big, strong, adult men. However, with lightweight, easy-to-use firearms readily available—big and strong are no longer necessary.

Even a young child can carry, and use, a gun.

Along with being able to handle guns and ammunition, children are also seen as both physically and emotionally vulnerable. They can be easily intimidated. In the case of abduction, it's commonplace for one of the abducted children in a group to be killed. This example sends a message to all of the others that if you try to escape or if you do not obey your commanders, you too will be killed. This is the "initiation." In fact, children are even sometimes forced to commit atrocities in their home villages, against friends and family, putting them in an even more desperate situation because they can never return home.

Child soldiers are often considered "cheaper" to keep. They eat less, they are more resilient and need less medical care (or at the very least are provided less care) and are much more predictable in their actions.

There is much global talk of nuclear conflict and "weapons of mass destruction." Lt. General (Ret.) Romeo Dallaire, commander of the UN forces in Rwanda in 1994 and now a Canadian senator, uses that same language when talking about the use of child soldiers. "Children have become the new weapons system," he explains. "They're not high-tech, but they are weapons of

Fires are a constant threat to families in the internal displacement camps.
The tarped huts are evidence of recent fires in the region.

mass destruction. How do you fight a war against children?"

That question alone, is a moral dilemma that may never have any answers.

Human rights organizations worldwide are working with the United Nations and individual countries to end the use of child soldiers. Much work is also being done to support child soldiers after the end of their time in conflict. Regardless of the length of time as active participants in war, the trauma is life-altering. The current stream of support is through Demobilization, Disarmament and Reintegration (DDR) programs that are focused on providing psycho-social support, along with education,

training and skills for these children so they can make an attempt at life back home in their communities.

While these DDR programs do exist, there are too few of them worldwide. And when they do exist, they lack the resources necessary to provide for the needs of these now incredibly vulnerable returnees. More often than not, these children are left on their own to cope with a childhood lost and a level of trauma few can even begin to comprehend. These soldiers are above all else, simply children, who continue to suffer from the effects of the wars they have been forced to fight.

ANNU

Born in a War Zone

Annu woke to the sounds of gunfire. It wasn't unusual, and that was part of the tragedy of her life. War was all she'd known. Since the time of her birth her country had been at civil war, and conflict was as much a part of her life as the hugs of her mother.

But today it seemed different. It wasn't just a few shots and it didn't seem to be stopping. In fact it was getting more frequent and, more frighteningly, louder and closer. She knew she had to act.

She rolled from her bed—the bed she shared with her mother. She called out for her mother, but there was no answer. She was alone. She knew her mother could have gone to the market or was at the home of a friend or family member. While she was worried about being alone, it wasn't that unusual; Annu wasn't a baby, she was almost seven years old.

She was old enough to know that she needed to seek cover, not run out to find her mother. Her mother would take shelter and she had to do the same—but where?

She tried to stop her heart from pounding so loud. She tried to slow her breathing and her thoughts. She needed to listen. She needed to think. She listened for the sounds of the gunfire. She had enough experience to know that it was guns or rifles, and not coming from a helicopter or aircraft. That was important. What type of gunfire determined where she should flee. If it was fire coming from the sky she would head to the bunker, the little covered trench behind her house; but if it was coming from the ground she had to get out of the house but avoid the bunker. It was hidden from the sky, but any soldiers walking along the ground would easily find it—and find her.

Annu knew she had to find a place to hide. For a few seconds

Annu on her 5th birthday.

she stood there, frozen in place, thinking about her mother, hoping she was safe, but also thinking about where she needed to go to find safety as well. She realized that she couldn't help her mother, but there was somebody she could help. Lying in the corner of the small room, sleeping on an old blanket, was her cat, Kutti. Kutti wasn't very big. It was just a gray-and-white ball of fur, but she loved Annu and Annu loved her cat. She grabbed Kutti in her arms and ran outside.

Annu's house was small. Her parents had planned to make a bigger house, but then the war broke out. There wasn't any point in building something that might be destroyed or damaged one day. A larger house would have to wait until there was peace. They'd been waiting a long time.

The property itself wasn't much bigger than the house. It was rocky rough ground, and they couldn't plant crops. Only the Palmyra trees grew. It was the leaves of these trees that formed the roof of their house and the fence that surrounded the property. Among the trees was a gigantic haystack. Her grandparents, who lived just a few houses away, had left the stack there to

Annu and her first cousins. Annu sits in the middle wearing a pink dress. Six of her cousins now live in Canada, the rest are in India, London, England, and Sri Lanka (Colombo).

feed their livestock. This was the place Annu would hide.

She made her way to the haystack, Kutti in her arms. The haystack sat closer to the road than her home, but she hoped it would be safe. Any soldiers walking down her drive would go to the house and then to the bunker to search.

As she walked she stroked the cat and quietly talked to it. Maybe she was trying to reassure Kutti. Probably she was trying to reassure herself. The gunfire got louder and louder. Whoever was out there was waging a battle. She knew on one side would be members of the Tamil Tigers and on the other either government troops or maybe members of the Indian Army—people who had been sent in to create peace but now were

just another part of the conflict. If the Tamil fighters won and drove away the other side, she knew she'd be safe. She hoped she'd be safe. A stray bullet, once fired, didn't ask who it hit or who it killed. Civilians, little children, didn't have to be the intended target to be the ones killed. She knew the stories. She knew the victims. Adults, women, old people and children, even babies, had been caught in the deadly cross fire and had their lives ended.

Hiding behind the haystack she felt safer but scared and vulnerable. It was such a big pile that it certainly hid her from anybody passing on the road, but she knew that hay wouldn't stop a bullet. She also knew that she was simply behind the stack and that a soldier walking through the front gate and down the driveway would see her. She needed to burrow into the stack of hay.

Kutti was just a stray. Annu wasn't sure if she found the cat or the cat found her. What she was sure of was how much she loved the cat, and she knew it cared for her too. They had a special bond, and Annu loved to stroke the cat as much as the cat loved to be stroked. When it saw Annu it would run toward her, perhaps hoping for a small treat that sometimes came, but more just wanting to be petted, to be shown love and affection. In some ways cats are very much like people.

But now, as she tried to burrow into the straw, her cat was not happy. It clawed at her arms, trying to get free. And as determined as Kutti was to get free, Annu was determined to keep it safe.

"Hold still!" she whispered at the cat as it continued to struggle. "If the soldiers see you, they will shoot you!"

Annu didn't know the soldiers. Whether they were Indian—and Hindu, like most of the Tamils—or government soldiers, she only knew to fear them. She and her mother had been taken from buses and searched and questioned and their identification checked. And she would just stand there, clutch her mother's hand, bury her face in her side, hoping that the stories she'd heard

weren't about to happen to her—people taken to jail by the soldiers to be tortured or killed, or shot right there at the side of the road.

She'd heard the story of a little boy, no older than her, who was shot dead because the soldiers heard him sing a song celebrating the Tamil Tigers. She hadn't been there but she'd heard the stories. Everybody knew. Even small children. There were always lots of stories.

What she had seen with her own eyes were people being yelled at, pushed in the back with guns, pulled off the buses and put in the backs of jeeps to be taken to places she had no way of knowing—was it jail...was it torture...was it to be killed? Her imagination was left to fill in the blanks. She had heard the cries of her neighbors and her family members, crying over the death of somebody they loved who was now gone. One story stood out vividly in her memory.

A neighbor, a good friend of the family, had come back from the funeral of her daughter. The daughter had been a member of the Liberation Tigers of Tamil Eelam (LTTE). Annu had remembered the fighting the day before, and it was in that battle that the neighbor's daughter had been killed. Only a few had been allowed to see the body before the funeral because the head had been severed. The whole village had come to the neighbor's home to pay respect to the family. And all night, long after dark had fallen and the people had gone home, Annu could hear the mother crying. She thought that the mother sounded like a wounded animal. It went on and on, keeping Annu awake. It was the last sound she heard before she finally managed to get to sleep.

Kutti's claws raked Annu's arm. Her first urge was to just release it. Her second was to strike it for hurting her. She did neither. She held it more firmly with the one hand while she continued to bury them both in the hay, using her body as a little shelter to protect the cat. She used all her power, pinning the cat against her in such a way that it couldn't escape. She was not going to let her cat suffer the fate of other pets.

Annu had a good friend who lived not far. They were schoolmates. Her friend had a dog. It was a nice dog. It lived outside, tied to a stake. It was a pet, but it also was a watchdog. It would bark when people came, warning them of visitors or strangers. Warning them of danger.

Her friend and her family had heard the plane up above and knew they had to flee their home. Sometimes the planes dropped bombs, or gunfire spewed out and hit people on the ground. The noise was getting louder and louder, and they ran, stumbling, jumping into the little bunker behind their house. That bunker, like most, wasn't much more than a ditch, as high as their heads, covered at the top, sometimes with metal and then a layer of Palmyra leaves to disguise it so it couldn't be seen from the air. The whole family scrambled in and pulled the roof into place.

There was no doubt that Annu and her mother were in a similar hole in the ground on that night. In some strange way Annu liked the bunker. The walls were only made of dirt and the bottom often held a a few inches of rainwater, but it seemed so much safer than their house. Here the walls were the earth itself and bullets couldn't penetrate. Of course nothing could stop a bomb being dropped from above, and Annu had seen the walls shake—felt the ground shake—when a bomb hit close by. She'd even heard of families who had been buried in their bunkers as the sides collapsed. She tried not to think about any of that.

For her friend that night it felt like the bombs were dropping almost on top of them. And it wasn't just one blast, but a second and a third and a fourth. They all huddled together, waiting, praying, hoping, and then it stopped. No more blasts. And as they listened, the sound of the airplane faded away and was gone completely. They lifted the leaves, pushed the roof aside and climbed out. Now that they were safe they hoped their house was safe. They moved slowly, still listening. The house remained—the walls and the roof were intact.

Then the family saw the dog. The collar was still around its neck, the rope still pegged to the ground, but the dog was dead. There was no doubt. It was ripped in two, half still tied up, the other half a dozen feet away.

Annu hadn't seen it, but the image was so strong in her mind that she'd never forget it. And, she would never let this fate be that of her Kutti.

The cat had given up the struggle. Partly because Annu had it so tightly pinned to her body that it had no room to struggle, but partly, she hoped, because it knew that she was there to take care of it. Then Kutti started to call out. The first plaintive cry had almost startled Annu.

"Be quiet," she hissed at the cat. "Don't shout out…you might get us both killed!"

She put her hand over the cat's mouth. It still made little sounds but it wasn't able to screech anymore. Now she had one hand to hold the cat and the second to hold its mouth closed. There was no hand free to stroke the cat anymore. She looked down.

DEMOCRATIC SOCIALIST REPUBLIC OF SRI LANKA

Population: 22,200,000
Location: Latitude: 7° N, Longitude: 81° E, an island in the Indian Ocean south of India
Area: 65,600 square kilometers
Climate: tropical, monsoon
Languages: Sinhala (Official and National language) 74%
Tamil (National) 18%
Other 8%
English (used by 10% of the population)
Ethnicity: Sinhalese 74%
Moors 7%
Indian Tamils 4.6%
Sri Lankan Tamils 3.9%
Others 10%
Religion: Buddhist 70%
Muslim 8%
Hindu 7%
Christian 6%
Life Expectancy: 73 years
Infant Mortality Rate: 13 deaths per 1,000 live births
Per Capita Income: $4,600
Literacy rate: 92% (male 94%, female 92%)

Annu's mother had a camera; she used to dress up Annu for pictures.
Annu's grandfather is in the background.

The little cat looked scared. She was scared too, but then she realized that Kutti was afraid of her! Kutti didn't know why she was doing this, why the little girl who had always treated her so nicely was now hurting her. The cat didn't know why, it just knew that it was happening.

In some ways the cat and the little girl had a lot in common. Annu didn't really know why the war was happening. She didn't know about the big issues, about politics, or peace or world opinion. All she knew was that her family was Tamil and that people she knew and loved were being killed. People she knew had become members of the Tamil Tigers, and she was told they were fighting for her, fighting for her future. When they won a battle, the streets were filled with people cheering. There were loudspeakers playing patriotic songs that celebrated Tamil fighters.

Gradually the gunfire became less frequent, and then it stopped altogether. Annu stayed in the haystack a little bit longer. She knew that it was best to wait, to be safe and make sure it wasn't just at a lull but at an end. Finally satisfied she pushed aside the straw and stepped into the daylight. She released her cat and before she could reach down to reassure it that everything was safe it ran off, racing between the trees, around the side of her house and disappeared.

Now it was safe for her to go back to the house and wait for her mother to return. Or maybe it would be a cousin sent to get her or an aunt or maybe one of her grandparents. She hoped it was her mother. Then Annu would know her mother was safe. That was the most important thing, her mother, because her father wasn't there anymore.

Annu's father, like so many men in the village, had fled the country. They didn't want to be killed by the army. All they wanted was a safe life for their families, and they'd left the country to try to establish a life, get a job, create a home and take their families away from this war. Annu's father had left when she was less than two. He returned to the family for short visits, but mainly his picture was the most she knew of him. Someday, her parents had promised, they would all be together, and it would be in a place where they didn't have to fear for their lives, a place that would be safe.

Annu was told stories, and promises were made. Those stories were just that—stories. Was there actually a place where people didn't have to live in fear, where gunfire didn't punctuate the day, where families lived together in peace? She hoped, but she didn't know.

Right now she was just worried about her mother coming home. And she thought about her cat, the way it had run away from her, the look in its eyes when she was just trying to save its life. It didn't understand why she was treating it so roughly. Annu understood. She had no choice, but the cat didn't understand.

Annu's mother returned shortly after. Kutti was never seen again.

Follow-up: Annu

Annu and her mother left Sri Lanka to be united with Annu's father. The family ultimately immigrated to Canada. Annu is now twenty-two years of age and recently graduated from university.

Jaffna

Colombo

Sri Lanka

History

Sri Lanka is an island country located in the Indian Ocean, just south of India. It contains an ancient civilization with continuous documented settlement for close to three thousand years. It existed as a number of independent kingdoms or territories for most of this time period.

While always closely intertwined with the Indian Subcontinent, the northern part of the island was, at one point, seized by a southern Indian dynasty, and a Tamil Kingdom was established.

It came under the influence of various European countries, beginning with the Portuguese in the sixteenth century, then the Dutch in the seventeenth century, and the island was ceded to Britain in 1796. The entire island was united under British rule

in 1815 and was called Ceylon. It was considered valuable not only for the warm climate and fertile fields that produced numerous crops—especially tea—but also because of its strategic position in the sea lanes.

With even greater potential for agricultural uses, the British imported from southern India close to one million Indian Tamils to work in the large-scale plantations. This created a "visitor" population that was closely related to the Sri Lankan Tamils but considered by many, especially the majority Sinhalese population, as not truly being Sri Lankan.

The British Empire controlled countries and people around the world. The people in various countries, including India to the north and Ceylon, began asking for more rights and freedoms. In 1948 Ceylon became an independent country with citizens being given the right to vote for their government.

With the right to vote, there were fears in the minority communities that the majority group, the Sinhalese, would establish dominance to such a degree that the rights of the minorities would be reduced or impinged. There was an acknowledgment that the government would protect minority rights and recognize the country as being pluralistic in nature.

The Sinhalese, who spoke Sinhala and were almost exclusively

A tea plantation in Sri Lanka. Tea accounts for almost 25% of Sri Lanka's export earnings.

Buddhist, composed almost 75 percent of the population. The Tamils were composed of two groups, Indian and Sri Lankan Tamils, and they combined to form the largest minority group. They spoke Tamil as their primary language and were mainly Hindu, but had a significant number of Catholics as well. A third group, the Moors, was Muslim. While all three groups lived throughout the country, the Tamils formed a majority of the population in parts of the north and east of the country.

The dreams of a pluralistic country, representing all groups, quickly dissolved once independence was reached. One of the first acts of the government was to disenfranchise

the Indian Tamils, removing their right to vote. This was done despite the fact that the vast majority of these people were born in Sri Lanka, as were their parents and, in some cases, their grandparents.

Subsequently, Sinhala was made the official language of the newly formed country, contrary to an understanding that Tamil was also going to be recognized as an equal language.

Leaders in the Tamil community attempted to undertake political action to get the language recognized and to receive more rights and freedoms, especially in areas where the Tamils formed the majority. These efforts were not just supported in their community but by moderate members of the Sinhalese community. But, there were also members of this community who strongly opposed the extension of minority rights. There was both political protest and violence against the moderates. The most extreme example of this occurred in 1959, when the prime minister, who was Sinhalese and wished to extend further minority rights, was assassinated by a Buddhist monk.

Continued efforts by good people in both communities to resolve these issues to allow minority rights to be protected were continually thwarted by extreme elements in both communities. Some Tamils simply wanted complete Tamil independence and would not consider anything less. Some Sinhalese wanted complete domination and would accept nothing less than Sri Lanka being considered a Sinhalese-Buddhist state. These extreme positions and people continually pushed the moderate majorities on both sides, and peaceful attempts to a political solution were unsuccessful. This situation combined with historical factors were the precursors for the eruption of a civil war.

The Conflict

Seeing no progress in the peaceful process of negotiation, some members of the Tamil community became more open to elements who believed that violence was the only solution. Various groups evolved under different leadership, but ultimately one organization, the Liberation Tigers of Tamil Eelam (LTTE), became the dominant military group. It was advocating for protection of Tamil rights and freedoms, a desire to create a semi-autonomous province within Sri Lanka or the creation of a completely separate Tamil nation in the areas in the north and east of the country where Tamils formed a majority of the people.

This group was funded by local Tamils, Tamils living abroad and sending back money, and, allegedly, by criminal activities that included robbing banks or government institutions.

While this conflict had been ongoing in some form for many years, the civil war is thought to have been ignited by two significant incidents. The Sri Lankan prime minister was assassinated by a suicide bomber believed to be Tamil. On July 23, 1983, the Tamil Tigers ambushed and killed thirteen members of the Sri Lankan army. The reaction involved mobs attacking and killing Tamils. Vehicles were stopped at intersections, and if the occupants were Tamils, the vehicle and people were set on fire. Tamil houses were set on fire, looted or destroyed. There are different accounts of the number of people killed and homes destroyed. Estimates range from 400 to 3,000 deaths with 1,000 being generally accepted as a reasonably accurate number. There were between 10,000 and 18,000 homes destroyed, and the first mass exodus took place as tens of thousands of Tamils left the south and fled to the north, where Tamils felt safe. This has come to be known as Black July and is commemorated by the Tamil community every year through peaceful demonstrations around the world.

Some members of the Tamil community believe that the mobs were instigated by the government. While there is no credible and certain proof to support these allegations, it is clear that policemen and soldiers stood by in the early stages and did not attempt to stop the violence or protect the victims and their homes.

The conflict between the Sri Lankan forces and the forces of the LTTE originated as a battle between a regular military force and a guerilla group. The government forces were much more numerous, had the support of aircraft, heavy equipment and greater weaponry. They were supported by the majority Sinhalese population and controlled the vast majority of the country.

The LTTE utilized guerilla techniques, including ambushes, roadside bombings, suicide bombings and assassinations. These techniques resulted in the deaths of many civilians and innocent victims as well as members of the government forces.

As the civil war continued, the LTTE became better equipped, better trained and began engaging the Sri Lankan army in regular combat. They drove out government forces in sections of the north and east, effectively creating a separate and autonomous Tamil state.

The government responded to this by sending overwhelming forces, supported by aircraft, to attack the LTTE stronghold in Jaffna. It appeared that the siege and subsequent combat was on the verge of crushing the Tigers when India intervened in the civil war by using its highly superior air force to drop supplies to the Tamils, breaking the siege.

The role of the Indian government in its decision to intervene in another country's internal conflict was highly unusual. It was fueled by the facts that there were many Indian Tamils, that most Tamils are Hindu and that the southern part of India has a large Tamil population.

With the intervention of India, the conflict once again became a stalemate between the two forces. India then took the step, with cooperation of the Sri Lankan government, of sending in a large group of troops to those areas in the north and east where the conflict was taking place.

This group, known as the Indian Peace Keeping Force, was mandated to supervise and separate the groups, attempt to disarm the Tamil Tigers (LTTE) and protect the rights of the Tamil population.

What started as a humanitarian effort quickly degenerated, and violence began between the Indian Peace Keeping Force and the Tamil Tigers. This conflict lasted for 32 months, ending in March, 1990. In that time there were over 1,000 Indian soldiers and an estimated 4,000 Tamils killed. This violence even continued after the withdrawal of the troops, when an LTTE woman assassinated the former Indian prime minister, Rajiv Gandhi, in a suicide bombing.

With the withdrawal of the Indian Peace Keeping Force there was a power vacuum. The Sri Lankan government forces were not able to fill that gap, and rival Tamil factions fought, with the Tamil Tigers eventually taking control. They initiated many government services and, in essence, set up a temporary provisional government in some areas.

This shift also marked another phase, where battles erupted between Tamil and Muslim factions. It is estimated that up to twenty-eight thousand Muslims were forced to leave the Jaffna area in an instance of ethnic cleansing, moving south, fleeing in fear for their lives as homes and businesses were destroyed and people were killed. It was reported that burning bodies on the side of roads was a common sight. The government began again to use its troops and air force to bring the rebels under control. Aerial bombing was a constant threat to civilians throughout the area, and running gun battles between the Tamil Tigers and government forces often saw civilians and children as innocent victims caught in the cross fire.

In 2001, eighteen years after the commencement of the civil war, formal talks began about a cease-fire. This agreement, brokered by Norway, called for the government to drop its ban on the Tamil Tigers and allow a sharing of power and some regional autonomy. In exchange the Tigers were to drop their demand for an independent Tamil state. This agreement came into effect in 2002.

It is estimated that during the civil war over sixty-eight thousand people were killed, one million people were internally displaced within the country, and hundreds of thousands had left the country and were dispersed throughout the world.

The cease-fire was a temporary measure to allow the two sides to negotiate a lasting peace settlement that would satisfy all parties. While it started with hope and good faith, the negotiation process failed to find

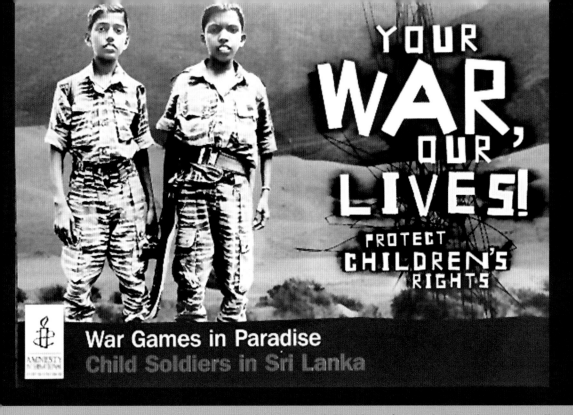

The cover of an Amnesty International letter shows two child soldiers of Sri Lanka's Tamil Tigers guerrilla movement (LTTE) sent as part of a campaign in Colombo against the LTTE's recruitment of children.

a solution and the cease-fire was broken on a fairly regular basis.

In 2006 the cease-fire was completely voided. In the first year of the resulting escalation of violence, it is believed that over 1,000 soldiers were killed and another 100,000 Tamils were displaced. The civil war is ongoing.

Tamil Tigers—Terrorists or Freedom Fighters?

The Liberation Tigers of Tamil Eelam (LTTE) have operated in some form since the early 1970s. They originated as a small group, one of many, which were attempting to seek protection for the Tamil minority and form either a semi-autonomous Tamil state within the country of Sri Lanka or an independent state in the north and east of the island. Originally this group was small, poorly organized and funded and practiced, almost exclusively, guerilla techniques in its fight against the government forces.

As the conflict became a full-fledged civil war in 1983, the Tigers became the dominant group representing the movement for Tamil independence. They had not only

37

a military wing but a political wing that had international contacts. The organization became larger with over ten thousand men and women, was better funded and better trained and acquired more sophisticated weaponry. While they continued to utilize guerrilla tactics, they were able to engage the Sri Lankan security forces in more conventional battles.

The Tigers, while seen as freedom fighters by many Tamils, have carried on activities that have also had them labeled as terrorists. These activities include the extensive use of suicide bombings that have resulted in the deaths of innocent civilians; targeting political figures for assassination, including a Sri Lankan prime minister and a former Indian prime minister; killing innocent civilians; the ethnic cleansing of Muslims in Jaffna; recruitment and use of child soldiers; and allegations of killing other Tamils who fostered other beliefs or supported other groups.

The Tigers have been listed as a terrorist organization by countries around the world, including India, the United States, the United Kingdom, Canada and the entire European Union. This label is strongly refuted by the organization and members of the Tamil community in Sri Lanka and around the world. They deny many of the allegations and defend certain actions as being the consequences of an ongoing war for their rights and freedoms.

Indian Connection

India is the giant to the north of Sri Lanka. It is the second largest country by population, having over one billion people, and the seventh largest by land mass. The two countries are connected by geography— Sri Lanka is an island just off the coast of India—and by history, both once being part of the British Empire and then becoming independent.

India is a highly diverse country that is primarily Hindu but has large populations of other religions, including the second largest Muslim population in the world. While the national language is Hindi, there are fourteen official languages and over 400 languages spoken in different parts of the country. The Tamil language is spoken by 61 million people in India, primarily in the south in the areas adjacent to Sri Lanka. This population dwarfs the Tamil population in Sri Lanka and is almost three times as large as the entire population of that county. At one point there was a dynasty that linked this population of Tamils with those in Sri Lanka, and during the reign of the British Empire, a million Indian Tamils were moved from India to Sri Lanka to work in the plantations.

India has always had an official or unofficial interest in Sri Lanka, which involved direct intervention—the airlift of materials into Jaffna and the Indian Peace Keeping Force—and indirect intervention, including allowing Tamil refugees to settle there, or allegations that they funded and trained Tamil independence factions.

India's involvement in Sri Lanka has had two primary interests that have been dictated by the reality of its large Tamil population. The country could not sit back and watch as Tamils were killed, which would risk inflaming their Tamil population, but it also feared that the formation of a separate Tamil nation in the north of Sri Lanka would inspire thoughts of independence in the Tamil population in India.

Religion

The four major religions of the world, Islam, Christianity, Buddhism and Hinduism, all are represented in this small island nation.

Buddhism: The Buddhist faith is practiced by over 300 million people throughout the world, with the largest concentrations being in Southeast Asia. It is 2,500 years old and is based on the teachings of Siddhartha Gotama. While it has been subdivided into three major factions, all ascribe to a belief centered on finding the Middle Way, a code of life that seeks moderation, tolerance and acceptance. One of the primary precepts is that adherents should refrain from the taking of life of any living thing.

Hinduism: It is the third largest religion in the world with over one billion adherents. It is centered on the Indian Subcontinent and the oldest of all major religions. It is based on the Vedas, texts which originated in ancient India. Within the religion is an acceptance that there are many gods and many diverse routes to salvation.

Islam: It is the second largest religion in the world with 1.4 billion adherents. It follows the teaching of the Qur'an, which was established by the Prophet Muhammad in the seventh century. It has two main subgroups, the Sunni and Shi'a sects. It is practiced throughout the world but centers in the Middle East.

Christianity: It is the largest religion in the world with 1.8 billion members. It is divided into three primary groups: the Roman Catholic Church, the Protestant movement and Orthodox Catholicism. All follow the teachings of the Bible and believe that Jesus Christ is the Savior, and his teachings in the New Testament form the basis of religious salvation and personal life.

Islam and Christianity, while in conflict in many areas around the world, share many common historical roots.

FAROOQ

Home Under Fire

Farooq climbed the stairs, shielding his eyes as he stepped out into the sunshine of the courtyard. It was so bright compared to the dim faint light of the basement. He stepped out and took a deep breath of air. It was clean and cool. Despite the clear brilliant sunlight with no clouds in the blue sky, it was still winter, and Kabul had cold winters. He was bundled up against the weather, but he still felt the chill against his face.

He looked up at their house. It was spacious and friendly—and now unoccupied. They could go inside during the day to retrieve things—if there was no sound of shelling—but they had abandoned their home and taken refuge in the smaller building. It was the only building with a basement and it sat inside the courtyard of their home so it was more protected.

Being protected was important. All around the neighborhood—all around the entire city of Kabul—houses had

been hit by rockets and cannons and tank shells and stray bullets. The capital of Afghanistan, Kabul was a bustling place of businesses, factories, markets and mosques and was home to over a million people. Now, all across the city, people were being killed and homes were being destroyed as rival mujahideen groups fought to gain control.

Of course, Farooq, who was five, didn't know about this conflict. He just knew that things were different for his family and in his neighborhood. His father, a successful businessman, mostly stayed home. Farooq didn't go to school. They slept in a basement, cooked in the garage and didn't venture out of their neighborhood. Even then, the war had come to them.

Just down the street was a small bakery. His mother would prepare dough for bread, and one of Farooq's jobs was to take the dough down the street to be baked. He was proud to be of help to his family, and since

Afghan children walk past the war-damaged Darlaman Palace in Kabul. Sixty-three thousand homes and more than 60% of the streets were damaged in over two decades of conflict.

everybody in the neighborhood knew each other there was no danger in him being out alone even at his age.

There was always somebody out walking or sweeping, adults gathering together to talk or looking out windows. There were always friendly eyes watching out for all the children. Afghanis are famed not just for their hospitality but for their love and caring for children.

As Farooq walked back from the bakery that day, carrying the bread, he briefly stopped by the park on his street. Today there were no children playing. The big rock in the center was empty. He'd been told not to climb it anymore. It was a high spot where he could see out but also where he could be seen. It was dangerous to be seen from a distance. He hurried on his way.

Suddenly there was a loud swooshing sound and an explosion. Farooq screamed and tossed the bread into the air as he was splattered by mud and dirt. Momentarily stunned, he ran for home, finding his mother and throwing himself into her arms.

Her first question was about the bread and what had happened to it, before she realized how close she had come to losing her son. She held him tightly, and he held on, feeling safe in her arms.

The little basement certainly wasn't home, but Farooq's mother had done all she could to make it comfortable. They had taken carpets and beds down into the small basement. And between those things and the fire, it was warm and comfortable and kept out the cold winter nights. Together, he and his parents and sister and aunt and cousin slept in the little room.

Farooq missed sleeping in his own room, but part of him liked them all being together. If he woke up in the night he could hear the breathing of the others, and in the light of the fire peeking out of the cracks in the woodstove, he could see the sleeping shapes of his mother and father. Those sights made him feel safer.

"Farooq, come," his father said. He was carrying three water jugs.

Instantly Farooq fell in beside his father. He was an obedient boy, but he also just liked being with his father.

Getting water was a daily task. The house had taps and running water, but that had stopped working weeks before. It and the electricity were the first casualties of the fighting. Luckily for them there was a working tap just a few houses up on the street.

As they walked Farooq held onto an edge of his father's coat. He'd been doing that a lot lately—since the explosion that had come so close to him on his walk home from the bakery. He just felt better to be right there by his father's side. When Farooq had first started to do that, his father had brushed him away, but now he knew it was important for his son to be close, that he needed to be close.

As they approached they saw that there was a lineup waiting to get water. That was often the case.

They settled into the back of the line, and his father began talking to the others who were waiting. He knew everybody and everybody knew him. They lived in a big city, but mainly they lived in their own little neighborhood. Almost everybody lived close by, used the same stores and businesses, gathered on the streets and the parks and worshipped at the local mosque. They were neighbors, but in some way they were like a larger extended family, many of them living side-by-side for many generations.

The men placed their water containers on the ground in a little line, and they clustered together in groups. Some squatted down, while others stood. Many smoked cigarettes, and they all exchanged stories about what was going on in the city.

Farooq was too young to understand much of what they said, but some things seemed clear even to a boy of his age. There might have been some laughter, but the men were mainly somber and serious. Whatever was happening wasn't good. He heard stories about people—people in the neighborhood—being wounded, or even killed. They talked about families who had left. They had gathered whatever they could carry, or put in their cars or carts, and abandoned their houses, going to stay with family in another part of the country where the fighting had passed or hadn't happened.

Farooq knew of people who had left. Some of the friends he'd played with, the mates from his school, were gone. Now he mainly played with his cousin and his little sister—two years younger and not much of a playmate.

Farooq was afraid of the bombs, but the last thing he wanted to do was leave his home and all his things behind. This was the only place he'd ever lived, the only place he'd ever known. But he also knew that he had no choice. He would simply go wherever his father decided was best.

"It was bad enough when we were being killed by foreigners," one of the men in line said to another. "But now it is Afghanis killing other Afghanis."

"A bullet doesn't care about the nationality of the person it hits," another man said.

"But it shouldn't be fired by one Afghani at another," the first protested.

"A Russian bullet or an Afghani bullet kills the same."

"I just prayed that when the Russians were forced to leave that it would be different," the first man said.

Farooq's father just shrugged. He was not a political man. He was a businessman. He had lived through the invasion of the Russians the way his ancestors had lived through invasion by the British, and before that, Darius, Genghis Khan, Tamerlane and Alexander the Great. The greatest

AFGHANISTAN

Population: 32,000,000

Location: Latitude: 33° N, Longitude: 65° E, southern Asia

Area: 647,000 square kilometers

Climate: cold winters, hot summers, arid to semi-arid

Languages: Afghan Persian (Dari) (Official) 50%

Pashtu (Official) 35%

Turkic languages 11%

Ethnicity: Pashtun 42%

Tajik 27%

Uzbek 9%

Religions: Sunni Muslim 80%

Shi'a Muslim 19%

Other 1%

Life Expectancy: 44 years

Infant Mortality Rate: 157 per 1,000 live births

Per Capita Income: $800

Literacy Rate: 28% (male 43%, female 12%)

armies in history had invaded Afghanistan over the centuries, but none had ever been able to tame or control it for long. The Afghanis were strong and tough and prided them-selves on their independence. They had always thrown out invaders and reclaimed their country. And now with the latest invaders expelled, a civil war was taking place as different sides tried to fill the power vacuum left behind by the retreating Russians.

Slowly they had moved up the line; now it was their turn. His father filled three water containers, giving the first to Farooq to carry. As they started to walk, Farooq held onto his father's coat with one hand.

"Use both hands for the container," his father said. "If you spill it you'll be going back by yourself to fill it."

Farooq did what he was told. He *did* need both hands to carry the heavy container.

"There's nothing to worry about," his father said to him.

"What?"

"There's no need for you to worry," his father repeated. "I'll make sure my family is safe."

They dropped off the water in the garage. This was their kitchen now, the place where meals were prepared. Sometimes they ate in there. Sometimes in the courtyard, when the weather allowed. Other times, especially when there was the sound of shelling or bullets, they ate in the shelter of the basement.

His mother was already in the garage preparing breakfast. Farooq put down his water container and quietly went back outside before he could be given more work to do. Carrying water was one thing but helping to prepare breakfast was another.

As he walked outdoors, he reached into his pocket and pulled some marbles out. He had many toys and games, but playing marbles was one of his very favorite things to do. He stopped in a little patch of sunny dirt in the corner of the courtyard. He bent down and with his finger he drew a circle. He placed some of the smaller marbles inside—he was going to use the larger one, his lucky marble, to knock the others out.

"Can we play?"

It was his cousin and his sister. Playing marbles with his cousin was one thing, but his sister, Zakia, only three, was too young to do anything except cause trouble. He wasn't posi-tive, but he thought she had actually swallowed some of his marbles before.

"You can play," he said to his cousin. "And she can watch," he continued, pointing to his sister.

She sat down on the ground. She didn't seem too disappointed. She was just happy to be around her big brother.

Farooq handed his cousin one of the big marbles. The idea of the game was to take the big marble and "flick" it so that it hit the little marbles in the circle. If you knocked out one of the little marbles, then it was yours. Some the bigger kids played it for "keeps." They got to keep whatever marbles they knocked out of the circle. For Farooq and his cousin, they just did it for fun. They were, after all, just kids, and playing was what they wanted to do. And while they were playing, they forgot everything else—all those things that were happening out beyond their home.

They kneeled down in the dirt beside the circle and took turns. His cousin was good, but Farooq was better. More than half the time he hit one of the little marbles and most of the time it skittered out of the circle.

Suddenly the quiet was broken. There was a loud sound—like an engine—and Farooq looked up. Just over their heads streaked a silver shape, a rocket! There was a loud *shoooshing* sound as it passed over, and then a tremendous explosion!

Farooq jumped to his feet and started to run before he heard the screaming. He stopped and turned back around. His cousin was cut, blood pouring from his face, and his sister was lying in the dirt, facedown, blood coming from her back!

His mother and father ran over, screaming, and scooped the children up and carried all three down to the basement. Quickly his parents looked at the injuries. Both children had been hit by debris thrown up in the air when the rocket had landed—maybe it was bits of rock or concrete. There was blood—coming from the nose of his cousin, and from a small wound on his sister's back—but the injuries were minor. It took longer to calm down his sister than it did to clean out the wound. She'd be fine. They'd all be fine...for now.

Follow-up: Farooq

Farooq, his mother, father and sister left their home. They walked for two days in the cold and rain, narrowly avoiding death, with only the possessions they could carry, to travel out of Kabul and to the home of a relative. Over 25,000 people, mainly civilians, were killed, and one-third of the city was completely destroyed.

Subsequently the family immigrated to India in 1996, and then to Canada in 1998, where his youngest sister, Rabia, was born. Farooq has recently graduated from high school and is taking further courses to prepare him to pursue a career in either business or law enforcement. He is proud of both his Afghani heritage and his Canadian future.

AFGhANIStan

History

Afghanistan has been home to human settlement for over 50,000 years and was one of the first documented places where farming took place. It is at the crossroads of Asia and has been referred to as the gateway between Asia and Europe. It has been continually exposed to travelers, traders, invaders and conquerors. It was conquered by Darius of Babylon in 500 BC, Alexander the Great in 329 BC, Islamic conquerors in the 7th century, Muhmujd of Ghazni in the 11th century, Genghis Khan in the 13th century, various Arab and Persian dynasties (including Tamerlane from Persia), the British Empire in the 1800s and the Soviet Union from 1979–1989. Throughout these recurrent invasions, the Afghan people have repeatedly demonstrated a fierce sense of independence, which has made it almost

impossible to effectively control and govern them. In all cases they have eventually expelled all invaders and conquerors.

This same quality of independence has made it very difficult for Afghans to govern themselves. The country we now recognize as Afghanistan has only existed in its present boundaries for the last part of its lengthy history. When not under the domination of outside powers, it has mostly existed as a number of independent or semi-independent countries, states, kingdoms, tribes or clan groups, which have either peacefully coexisted or actively battled each other.

In 1746 the Pashtun tribes were united into one group. They ultimately conquered and created a greater Afghanistan that was composed of all of the present-day Afghanistan, Pakistan, two provinces in Iran and parts of India. This greater Afghanistan came into conflict with the British Empire, the greatest power of its day and the largest empire ever amassed.

There were repeated conflicts between the two groups (1838–42, 1878–80, 1919–21). The British found that, while they could have initial success in these wars, the Afghans were not easily subdued or defeated. Great battles with heavy losses, retreats and re-entrenchments taking place—with the Afghans regaining lost territory—was the pattern. Cease-fires, treaties and accords were ultimately created that gave Britain some marginal control over Afghanistan's foreign policy but no real control over the majority of the people or the country.

In 1921 Afghanistan was granted independence from Britain. Emir Amanullah founded a monarchy in 1926. This kingdom remained in some degree of control throughout the country for almost fifty years, although there were continual internal power struggles, and many areas of the country operated as almost independent states.

In 1973 the king was deposed, and the monarchy was replaced by a republic. This set off another period of turmoil as different groups attempted to gain power. In 1978 the republic was overthrown, and a Marxist government with close ties to the Soviet Union was formed.

There was a great deal of internal resistance to this government and its official secular policy, as almost all Afghans are Muslim. This resistance became so strong that it appeared that the government would fall.

Soviet Involvement 1979–1989

There is debate as to whether the government of Afghanistan invited the Soviet Union to send troops to support it or the Soviets simply invaded. In September, 1979, its forces crossed their shared border and launched a massive invasion of Afghanistan. The existing leader of the country was killed, and another leader was installed by the Soviets as the president of Afghanistan.

The local groups who had fought against the previous Afghan government became even stronger in their opposition to the Soviet invaders. The resistance fighters, the mujahideen, pledged a jihad, or holy war, to expel the invaders.

The Soviet forces numbered in the hundreds of thousands and were supported by tanks, the most sophisticated weaponry available at the time, attack helicopters, planes and missiles. The Afghan resistance was in scattered pockets, under different leaders who did not necessarily cooperate and were, in fact, at times hostile to each other. These groups were lightly armed, some with outdated guns from World War II, and operated on foot or on horseback. Regardless of the differences between the weaponry, the resistance demonstrated that same level of fierce independence and willingness to fight that has been the mark of Afghans throughout history. And while many resistance fighters were killed, they continued to inflict heavy losses on the Soviets. The Soviets discovered what all other previous invaders had learned: that while this country is possible to invade, it is incredibly difficult to subdue or control.

This invasion was during a time of great conflict between the Soviet Union and the United States of America so the Soviet incursion was protested by the western world and clearly identified as an invasion and not a request by the existing government for their involvement. This country, previously ignored by the western world, became the focus of the Cold War conflict.

Through Western covert—secret— programs the resistance fighters were provided with sophisticated arms, training and intelligence that allowed them to continually evolve into a more effective, cohesive and dangerous foe. Attempts to expand Soviet and government control into areas outside of the capital, Kabul, were met with time-limited success and came at the cost of many deaths and casualties.

Along with Afghan fighters, there were calls for Muslims to come from other countries to continue the jihad against the Soviets. Among these outsiders was a Saudi man named Osama Bin Laden. It is alleged that he received training and funding from the Central Intelligence Agency (CIA) of the United States.

Equipped with increasingly sophisticated weapons, including portable missiles that could destroy helicopters, the resistance movement became more deadly as well as much more coordinated in its efforts. The war became increasingly violent as the Soviet army attempted to put down the uprising, and there were enormous casualties on both sides.

Those most affected though were the ordinary citizens. The ongoing war played havoc with the economy, destroyed infrastructure and made daily living, and even survival, impossible for millions of people. They fled their homes. It is estimated that close to five million Afghans fled their homes, either taking refuge in other parts of Afghanistan or leaving the country. Over a million refugees flooded into Pakistan and Iran, and hundreds of thousands settled in countries around the world.

As the war continued, it began to take a toll on the Soviet Union. The war was costing billions of dollars to pursue, including the cost of propping up the Afghan government. There was also an increasing loss of life. External world opinion, internal political pressure within the Soviet government as well as public disapproval continued to mount. The war was being fought at a terrible cost of money and men and, just as important, was beginning to appear to be hopeless.

After the Soviet Withdrawal 1989–1992

In 1989 an agreement was reached whereby the Soviet Union would withdraw its forces and the Western powers would stop providing support for the resistance fighters.

By the time the Soviets retreated from Afghanistan, they had suffered the loss of over fifteen thousand lives and many more times that number of wounded.

With the withdrawal of the Soviet forces, the Afghan government was in a very weak state. The various resistance groups which had already established control over large swaths of the country set up provisional governments in many rural areas. These groups had continued to fight the Afghan government, but some also started to negotiate and cooperate, and even battle other groups to position themselves to take control of the entire country. As the mujahideen continued to gain power throughout the country there became a feeling that the government would ultimately be defeated, and members of the armed forces began to plan how to cooperate with those who would eventually take power. In April of 1992, the government and the capital, Kabul, fell.

The Taliban

While there were various factions battling for control of the country, one group, the Taliban, slowly established a place of dominance. This group was defined by a very strict understanding of the practice of the Muslim faith. It imposed harsh fundamentalist laws, including stoning for adultery and severing hands for theft. There were public executions and beatings. Women were prohibited from work and school and had to cover themselves head to foot to go in public, and they couldn't go out without a male relative. Music and Internet were banned. Men were required to wear beards, and no public events, like soccer or kite-flying, were allowed. By 1998 they had effectively gained control of over 90 percent of the country.

The northern sections of the country remained in conflict with the Taliban. The Northern Alliance, as they came to be known, tended to be Shi'a Muslim while the Taliban were primarily Sunni. As well, the Taliban were mostly ethnic Pashtun, and the Northern Alliance belonged to other tribal groups.

The infrastructure of the country continued to be destroyed and the economy was weak. Infant mortality rates rose, life expectancy fell and people were not able to obtain the

An Afghan boy stands outside his tent in Kabul. Many families have been forced to relocate after fighting increased against the Taliban.

basics of life, including food, water or shelter. Millions of people, some who had returned home, once again fled either internally within the country or over to other countries.

During this period, the western world paid little attention to the internal battles within Afghanistan. There was no military involvement and very little foreign aid given to the country. While many countries were appalled by the strict interpretation of the Qur'an and the harshness of punishment and position of women, there were some things that were applauded. Afghanistan had always been a major world source of illegal drugs—opium and heroin—and this practice was almost completely

eliminated under the Taliban. Regardless, this country was now not seen to have any significant military value, and no countries intervened.

The Taliban in Power 1998—2001

Outside mujahideen had battled alongside Afghans to overthrow the Soviets and the communist government they had left behind. Once the Taliban established a government, these fighters were allowed to remain in the country. One of these groups, al-Qaeda, under the direction of Osama Bin Laden, saw little difference between the Soviet Union and the western world. In both cases they were seen as enemies of the Muslim faith. Al-Qaeda had the objectives of eliminating foreign influences on Muslim countries and eradicating infidels. The United States was seen as the primary enemy and attacks were planned. In 1993 a truck bomb exploded in the parking garage under the World Trade Center in New York City. In 1998 the American embassies in Kenya and Tanzania were bombed. In 2000 the destroyer USS *Cole* was attacked. As al-Qaeda became linked to this attack, the United States and the international community demanded the Taliban turn over the terrorists to international authorities. The Taliban government, which had been recognized by only a few countries in the world as the legitimate government, chose to ignore these demands. This was in part based on its lack of connection or willingness to be connected to the outside world, its belief that the international community would not act and finally, a strongly held Afghan obligation that these people were guests and that guests needed to be protected.

The United States, acting with the approval of many of its allies, launched a series of cruise missiles against al-Qaeda training camps in response to the bombing of the embassies. This action had very limited success and, in some ways, simply elevated this terrorist group in status and emboldened them by making them believe that the international community would not take significant actions.

September 11, 2001

The members of al-Qaeda had vowed to take the war across the ocean and strike at the United States on its territory. This threat became reality when four airplanes were hijacked on September 11. These planes crashed into both of the twin towers of the World Trade Center in New York, the Pentagon in Washington, DC, and the fourth plane crashed before reaching its target, also in Washington.

The initial reaction of this massive attack, which resulted in the loss of over two thousand lives, was stunned disbelief. Not since Pearl Harbor had there been such a massive and coordinated attack on American soil. And in this attack almost all the fatalities were civilians, including the indiscriminate deaths of women and children. In that instant the world community became galvanized, and the entire world condemned the loss of innocent human life.

The reaction of the world community was strong and instant. On September 18, the United Nations Security Council issued a resolution demanding that the Taliban turn over those people responsible for the September attack. The Taliban government requested proof of its involvement and again refused to follow this direction, but some attempts to negotiate through a third party were initiated. These attempts were seen as insincere by the western world.

While the political diplomatic process continued, members of the American and British Special Forces began to infiltrate Afghanistan and link up with the Northern Alliance, a group within the country which had been at ongoing war with the Taliban. On October 7, a massive aerial bombing campaign began, which targeted al-Qaeda training bases, military targets and airports. Next they targeted communication and control assets. While this barrage was militarily successful, there were undoubtedly large numbers of civilian deaths, and the country, already poor and lacking in infrastructure, was further weakened.

At the same time the Northern Alliance began a stepped-up campaign against the Taliban, attacking its positions. These attacks gained limited success until the Western powers directed air power against the Taliban positions, destroying equipment, killing fighters and providing accurate information to help direct the Northern Alliance attacks. By the beginning of November, the Taliban

forces were decimated, and the combined Northern Alliance forces surged through the lines and made their way to the capital. Kabul was taken and cities across the country fell from Taliban hands, with the brunt of its forces retreating to the southeast, surrounding the city of Kandahar.

All through the assault US Special Forces troops had been on the ground to assist the Northern Alliance. At the end of November, there was a major influx of US combat troops. By December the last of the Taliban and al-Qaeda forces were killed, subdued, went underground, or fled the country and took refuge in the mountain areas of Pakistan. Thousands of US and allied troops were now stationed in the country to try to provide a stable environment for the creation of an interim government.

In December, Hamid Karzai, a Pashtun and the leader of the Populzai clan, was named head of the interim government. In June, 2002, he formally became president. This position and his legitimacy were further confirmed in October, 2004, when the first elections were held and he was elected president.

The defeat of the Taliban, the ousting of al-Qaeda and the democratic election of a president have not, however, led to stability within the country. The US-led coalition continued to contribute large numbers of troops, equipment and expertise to support the government. It was highly questionable if the government could maintain order without the support of these external forces. Attacks have been continually launched on government forces, and large parts of the country remain under only marginal control of the central government.

In 2006 the US-led coalition was formally replaced by a UN-mandated force—the International Security Assistance Force (ISAF), which is composed of NATO countries. This was the first time that NATO, created for the defense of Europe, had operated outside of Europe.

Over 30,000 NATO soldiers, from thirty-seven countries, are in the ISAF and are serving in Afghanistan. They are in the country, with the approval of the government, to give assistance to the Afghanistan army to provide stability, fight Taliban and al-Qaeda forces and allow the government to retain power and create an environment for the country to be stabilized and rebuilt and to continue to develop.

In August, 2006, a major offensive involving Afghanistan and NATO forces was believed to have killed over two thousand Taliban fighters and once again provided a further opportunity for Afghans to govern themselves.

While the fall of the Taliban forces took place over six years ago, the coalition forces have discovered what all other previous armies had discovered: taking the country is difficult, but holding it is even more challenging.

NATO

The United States and the Soviet Union were allies in World War II, acting to defeat Nazi Germany. At the conclusion of the war, having defeated this enemy, the two former allies found themselves politically and ideologically opposed to each other. There were fears in Western Europe that the Soviet Union and its allies would turn against them. In response, the North Atlantic Treaty Organization was created in 1949. This was composed of Canada, the United States and ten European countries—the United Kingdom, Belgium, Denmark, France, Iceland, Italy, Luxembourg, the Netherlands, Norway and Portugal.

At the center of this treaty was an agreement that an attack on any country would be considered an attack on every country. This was considered a major deterrent to any of these countries being attacked by the Soviet Union or its allies.

In 1952, Greece and Turkey joined NATO. In 1955, West Germany was added and finally Spain in 1982.

With the breakup of the Soviet Union in 1991, the Warsaw Pact dissolved. In fact, many of the former Warsaw Pact members pursued democracy and asked if they could become members of NATO.

This shift in power left NATO without a purpose. There was no longer a clearly defined reason for its existence, and with the subsequent efforts of many former Warsaw Pact countries to pursue democracy, there was no longer a military force capable of challenging NATO in Europe. There were questions concerning the very purpose of NATO, and whether it should also be dissolved. However, it did have a distinct purpose in supporting and replacing UN forces in both Bosnia in 1995 and Kosovo in 1999 in the continued battles within the former Yugoslavia, in pursuing a policy of actively protecting human rights and creating an environment where peace could take root.

NATO's involvement in Afghanistan is the first instance where this organization has left Europe and taken on a very active role in another region. Its actions in Afghanistan are not so much in maintaining peace, but in actively fighting against an armed force and trying to destroy that enemy, and thereby create an atmosphere where Afghanistan can survive, rebuild and prosper.

It is significant that while Afghanistan is almost exclusively Muslim, all NATO members, with the exception of Turkey, are Christian countries. NATO's involvement has led to further claims by al-Qaeda and other Muslim organizations that it is, in some ways, a modern-day crusade against the Muslim faith.

Ethnic, Religious and Language Divisions

Afghanistan is almost exclusively Muslim, and the region is officially known as the Islamic Republic of Afghanistan. The vast majority of these Muslims, over 80 percent, are Sunni, while almost 19 percent are Shi'a. The conflict between these two groups has become very pronounced, even leading to deadly violence in many Middle Eastern countries.

The official languages of Afghanistan are Afghan Persian (or Dari), which is spoken as the first language of 50 percent of the population, and Pashtu, which is the first language of 35 percent of the population. Other languages, including Uzbek and Turkmen, make up the next largest language groups. There are more than a dozen other less popular languages, and many people speak more than one language, including either Afghan Persian or Pashtu or both.

Afghan women and children outside their tent in a camp for displaced people outside Kabul.

The largest ethnic group is the Pashtun, who make up over 40 percent of the population; the Tajik are over 25 percent, and large numbers of Uzbek and Hazara groups constitute almost 10 percent each. Historically these groups have been in conflict or have maintained a tentative peace while not integrating.

Poverty

Afghanistan has been one of the poorest countries in the world over the past one hundred years. The almost constant wars of the past thirty years have further destroyed the infrastructure of the country, killed hundreds of thousands of people, displaced millions, damaged its industrial base, hampered international trade and severely restricted farming and agriculture to the point where the country is not able to feed itself.

Recent mass influxes of capital and expertise since the overthrow of the Taliban regime have begun to reverse some of these trends, and progress is being made. However, this process is slow moving, and for many Afghans they do not see any progress or have a sense that their lives have improved. It remains a country with an extremely high infant mortality rate, high levels of illiteracy and low life expectancy, and millions of people have no, or limited, access to fresh water, reliable food supplies or guarantees of security in the face of ongoing conflicts.

NADJA

Life in Sniper Alley

Nadja turned over and opened her eyes ever so slightly. It was light, so the sun was up, but that didn't mean *she* had to be up. It wasn't like there was much of a reason to go out. There wasn't any school today—there hadn't been for months—and she wasn't even supposed to go outside.

She shifted around trying to get comfortable and get back to sleep, but she knew that wasn't really possible. Comfortable would have been in her bed in her room instead of on this thin mattress on the floor by the front door. It wasn't safe to sleep in her room. There was too much danger of the glass being shattered by an explosion or a stray bullet. Instead, her disturbed sleep was going to give way to an equally disturbing reality.

Outside the window lay the city that was her home—Sarajevo. It was a city of natural beauty. The Mijacka River ran through the core, and it was surrounded by heavily forested hills and majestic mountains, the Dinaric Alps.

It was these mountains that brought the world to Sarajevo in 1984, when it hosted the Winter Olympics. That was eight years ago when Nadja was only five, but she still remembered the atmosphere of the city during that time. Athletes and officials and tourists filled the streets, sightseeing, singing, sharing in the celebration of athletic excellence. In all there were 1,200 athletes from 49 countries, tens of thousands of officials, 10,000 volunteers and hundreds of thousands of visitors to the city.

The Olympics were recorded and broadcast around the world by almost seven thousand members of the media. They reported on the athletic events set against the backdrop of peace, goodwill, diversity and the beauty of the setting.

Nadja, aged 14.

All of Yugoslavia celebrated when one of their athletes, Jure Franko, won their country's first-ever Winter Olympic medal, the silver in the giant slalom.

Of course, that was before the war—before different regions separated from Yugoslavia. Back then Sarajevo was a city in the region of Bosnia in the country of Yugoslavia. Now it was the capital of the newly independent Bosnia-Herzegovina. And while of course the mountains still remained, they weren't home to winter sports but to the cannons and tanks and snipers that rained down death upon the city.

Nadja heard her mother moving around in the kitchen. Maybe it was time to get up. She knew her mother must be fixing breakfast, because she could hear her banging around. It might have just been her imagination, but Nadja thought that the less food that was available, the more noise her mother made when she was preparing it. She was making so much noise this morning that there wasn't much hope for what was being prepared.

Not that Nadja would complain. She didn't complain because she knew her parents did the best they could. As the siege continued, the food supply became less and less, not just the amount of food but the type of food. Nadja would have loved to have had some fruit...a banana or an orange would have been like a little piece of heaven.

While the lack of food had been difficult for everybody in the family, Nadja felt it was hardest on her eighteen-year-old brother, Sanel. It seemed like he was always hungry. Sometimes Nadja would try to get extra food just to give it to him. That was just like Nadja.

Nadja closed her eyes and thought about the sort of things they used to have for breakfast. She had a wonderful imagination, and she could picture them in her mind so clearly that she could almost smell the meal cooking, the aroma wafting through the air, and taste those tender...She opened her eyes again. There was no point in dreaming or imagining. Not when there were things to be done.

Nadja rolled off the mattress, stood up and stretched. She needed to get dressed and get ready for school... or at least what passed as school. She opened the door to her bedroom and cold air rushed in. It was like stepping outside. Most of the windows were gone, replaced by sheets of plastic. It served to keep out the rain and snow but couldn't keep out the cold. They didn't even bother to try to heat the room, and the walls were patterned with mould and mildew.

She opened the closet and removed the clothes she would wear that day. They were old and cold, but clean. At times there was water, but most often they had to carry it up the stairs—fourteen floors. And even then the electricity was off and washing had to be done by hand. Somehow despite these difficulties her mother always tried to make sure that they had clean clothes—just her way of trying to create a little pocket of normal in a world that was far from normal.

Nadja retreated to the bathroom to change. The little room was dark—there were no windows—and the little candle wasn't lit. She left the door partway open to allow in a little more light.

This little bathroom was also the room that the family would retreat to if there was artillery or gunfire. It was in the center of the apartment and, with no windows, offered the most protection. It wasn't safe—just safer.

In the corner was a large container of water. It had already been used for cooking and cleaning. Now, after it was used and reused for other things, it was eventually used to pour in the toilet to flush it.

Sometimes Nadja brought the water up to the apartment. One day she made seven trips up the two hundred and fifty-two stairs, each time carrying a ten-liter container.

It was so much easier when water just flowed up through the pipes.

Nadja gave both her mother and her father a kiss on the cheek and then a hug. It felt good to be wrapped up in her father's arms—warm and safe…at least as safe as she could feel anywhere. She thought back to a time when she believed that her father could protect her from anything. Now she knew better. Her parents tried to act brave, to pretend that they were safe, but Nadja knew better. She felt that the war had turned everyone into frightened children. Nobody could guarantee safety. It was safe for nobody, nowhere in Sarajevo.

Nadja sat down for breakfast. Once again her mother had been as much a magician as a chef. She had taken nothing and made it into something. Not like the old meals, but at least there was food on the table. She almost felt guilty for wanting more, for dreaming about it. This was enough and more than many people had.

Whatever food that entered the city had to come at a high price, either airlifted in by the United Nations or driven in by trucks while snipers shot at them, trying to kill the drivers.

Nadja didn't know the people in the hills and mountains that surrounded her city, but she knew what they were doing. They were trying to kill everybody who lived in Sarajevo.

BOSNIA AND HERZEGOVINA

Population: 4,500,000
Location: Latitude: 43° N, Longitude: 18° E, southeastern Europe
Area: 51,000 square kilometers
Climate: moderate with hot summers and cold winters
Languages: Bosnian, Croatian, Serbian
Ethnicity: Bosniak 48%
　　　　　　　　Serbian 37%
　　　　　　　　Croatian 14%
　　　　　　　　Other 1%
Religion: Muslim 40%
　　　　　　　Orthodox Christian 31%
　　　　　　　Roman Catholic 15%
　　　　　　　Protestant 4%
　　　　　　　Other/Non 10%
Life Expectancy: 78 years
Infant Mortality Rate: 10 deaths per 1,000 live births
Per Capita Income: $5,600
Literacy Rate: 97% (male 99% - female 94%)

They were doing it by firing bullets and by raining down tank and cannon shells onto the city.

Sometimes there were just a few shells—she could hear them whizzing overhead and then the explosions as they hit. Other times there were dozens and dozens of explosions, so fast and furious that there was hardly a break between the explosions. And then when things got quiet again, she could go outside and see the damage, the destroyed buildings. Some of those destroyed buildings were schools and churches. Others were water or power plants. That was why there were times with no electricity or water. Nadja had started to realize how you took things like that for granted until you didn't have them anymore. There was no electricity for cooking or to run the vacuum cleaner or washing machine or TV. And the water had to be carried up all those stairs because there wasn't electricity for the elevators.

Over the past six months Nadja had come to realize all these things. What she really didn't understand was *why* this was all happening. Why would people want to kill somebody they'd never even met? She wanted to know if those people in the mountains were happy when they were shooting and killing people.

And they did kill people. Everyday. Sometimes it was a sniper's bullet killing somebody as he walked down the street. Other times it was an explosion and dozens of people were killed or injured in just an instant. One minute a person would be standing in line waiting for bread, or gathering cherries or firewood, and the next moment she was lying dead in the street.

"Are you going to work today?" Nadja asked her mother.

"It's a work day, so I'm going to work."

Nadja knew what the answer was going to be before she even asked the question, but still she had to ask. Her mother was a business manager at the National Bank. Every workday she went down to the center of the city to work. Some days she could get a ride at least partway there. Most days she walked almost all of the twenty kilometers to and from the bank. And every day Nadja worried until she returned home.

"I'll be fine," she said.

"Did you listen for the reports?" her father asked.

Her mother nodded. The radio was their lifeline. A little transistor, powered by batteries, gave reports. In the old days—the days before the war—the radio might say where there had been a traffic accident or if the trolley was running on time or if there was snow coming. Now they gave updates on where the sniper activity was the worst. The radio reported which streets should be avoided, where the most shooting was taking place. Of course there were some streets that should always be avoided. The main street was called "Sniper Alley," and it was always crossed in a rush or hiding behind a vehicle for protection.

"I know which streets are safe," her mother said.

"Not safe," Nadja said. "Just *safer*."

"I'll be fine. Are you going to school today?" Nadja's mother asked.

"I wish I *could* go to school."

"I mean in the basement."

"If that's what you call it, then yes, I'll be going to school."

It wasn't safe for students to go to their regular school. Instead all of the children in the apartment building met in the basement to take lessons. Since they couldn't go to school, the school came to them.

Nadja liked school and she liked being able to be with friends, but she didn't like the basement. It was dark and cold and moldy. This was also the same place where everybody in the building went when the shelling got too bad: two hundred and seventy people all crowded together in three small underground rooms.

And if the shelling didn't stop, they all slept down there, lying on blankets, crammed together in that little space, all pretending that they

SARAJEVO

Population: 529,000
Location: Latitude: 44 ° N, Longitude: 18° E
Founded: 1263 AD but existed as a settlement since prehistoric times
Climate: moderate with hot summers and cold winters
Setting: Surrounded by the Dinaric Alps: the Miljacka River dissects the city.
Architecture: Old buildings, churches, mosques on steep narrow streets.

It was home to museums, art galleries, theaters, libraries and film festivals. Its residents included poets, painters, performers and Nobel Prize winners. It was referred to as the "Jerusalem of Europe" and people of Muslim, Catholic, Orthodox and Jewish faith all peacefully co-existed.

were sleeping, but really, hardly anybody did sleep. When they went down there at night, Nadja packed a bag with some crackers, playing cards and, of course, her teddy bear.

When the bombs hit close by, she could feel them, see the ceiling shaking, and she couldn't help but think about what would happen if one of those shells hit their building. The basement was the safest part of

Nadja in the ruins of the National Library, Sarajevo, summer 1996.

the building, but it couldn't protect them from a direct hit.

"Maybe you could bring down your guitar today," Nadja's mother suggested.

Nadja loved to play her guitar and sing. Before the war she was part of the famed children's choir, Palcici. This choir was just one example of the culture that was an integral part of Sarajevo.

And as much as Nadja loved to sing and play and perform, she was also a writer. She wrote poetry and kept a journal. These activities were as necessary for her as was food. Creativity was, by nature, part of Nadja's soul. But during the war, they also became an outlet, a way

for her to express her feelings, her fears, and to try to understand why these terrible things were happening. While she didn't necessarily have answers, she had questions and thoughts:

"I think you really only appreciate something when you lose it."

"Are those people in the mountains happy when they shoot and kill?"

"How can they do this and then look in the eyes of their own children?"

"For how long will my life consist of the dead space between two explosions?"

"I don't know how many more days will be scratched out of my life calendar."

For months now the children in the building had barely gone outside. They had school in the basement and played in the halls. They tried to never play too much on one floor—they didn't want to bother the tenants. What they wanted was to go outside and play... not to go too far or for too long... just to go outside—to ride a bike or go for an ice cream or play a game of tag. But everybody knew the dangers, so while they did some-times go outside, most of the time they stayed inside.

The radio and the newspapers carried stories and pictures. Every day there were people killed—waiting in line for bread, trying to get to work or gathering firewood. And Nadja heard the reports, read the papers, saw the pictures in the obituaries. Men and women and children, some older and some younger than her—all dead.

Some days were better and some were worse. On the bad days the snipers seemed to fill the air with bullets, and the shells were falling so quickly that there was hardly a gap between the explosion of one shell and the next. On one terrible day, over twenty thousand shells fell on the city.

On the best days, Nadja was allowed to venture outside, sometimes with her parents and sometimes just outside the building with her friends. That didn't happen too often. All of the children were pale because they mainly stayed inside.

Today had been strangely quiet. Nadja's sleep had been solid, undisturbed by shelling. There had been no explosions since she woke, and the radio hadn't reported any snipers in their area. There was beautiful sunshine pouring in through the kitchen window. Could today be a day she could venture out?

"Mama...could I go outside today?" Nadja asked.

Her mother didn't answer. She looked anxious and scared.

"It's quiet and I won't go far...just outside...just for a few minutes."

Nadja's father had just gone out.

It was up to her mother to make the decision alone.

"Please!" Nadja pleaded.

Her mother wanted her safe but knew that she couldn't keep Nadja inside forever.

"Just for a moment, all right?" her mother said.

Nadja raced out the door and down the stairs, taking each flight more quickly than the first. She felt like she was flying down the stairs. She ran outside and just stopped and stood there. The warmth of the sun against her face was so good. She felt like she was drinking the sun in through her skin.

Then everything changed. She wasn't sure if she heard the shell first or felt the vibration or was blinded by the smoke and dust that engulfed her. She staggered backward, rubbed her eyes and looked up. The front of her building was hanging there—a shell had hit her building! For a brief second she stood there, her mind not able to believe what her senses were telling her.

Then she ran for the building. She staggered forward, screaming, and then felt a sharp pain in her legs. She reached down...there was blood! She had been hit by the shrapnel! She kept running, reaching the door to the building and throwing her arms around a neighbor who was standing there.

It was like the whole world had changed. She was on the ground, and there was so much confusion. Dozens of neighbors gathered around her. Somebody pressed some towels against her leg to slow down the blood flow.

She could hear voices talking and screaming and crying, but she couldn't make out what they were saying as she started to drift in and out of consciousness. Then from all the voices she heard her father. He picked her up in his arms and pressed her tightly against his chest, her blood seeping into his shirt. Father and daughter were placed in a neighbor's car and rushed to the hospital.

"Dad, please don't let me lose my legs," Nadja whispered.

He held her tighter to his chest, offering her comfort, reassurances that he couldn't possibly know.

They arrived at the hospital and her father carried her inside, where Nadja was taken by a nurse and placed on a stretcher. All around her, on stretchers, and even lying on the floor, were other people who had been wounded—those waiting to be treated and those who were beyond treatment, those who were dead. Everywhere was chaos: people screaming in pain, crying, doctors and nurses rushing around trying to save the lives of those flooding the hospital.

Nadja tried to remain brave, but it was so hard waiting, not knowing, scared, fearful that she might lose her legs. She had heard about this happening to people. She knew what was possible.

Finally a nurse and a doctor came. They cut open her pants and examined her legs. The pain was so intense, shooting throughout her body. People around her were crying out in pain. She bit down on her lip, trying hard to stop herself from screaming out. Nadja looked down as her legs. She could see blood and places where the flesh had been ripped open. She could feel the pain. She could hear the screams and cries. But none of it seemed real. It was like she was watching it all happen, but that it wasn't happening to her, that it wasn't her life and legs that were at stake.

The doctor examined her legs. He said things to the nurse, things that Nadja didn't fully understand. What she did understand was that pieces of the shell—shrapnel—had penetrated her legs.

Nadja knew all about what could happen. She had heard about people who had been hit by shrapnel and had had to have their legs amputated—cut off. That was her greatest fear, even more than dying.

The doctor looked up at her. "You are a very lucky girl."

Nadja couldn't understand how he could possibly think that she was lucky. Unless…

"They all missed the bone. We'll clean the wounds, give you a tetanus shot and bandage you up, and we hope you'll be fine."

Now she wanted to cry for a different reason.

The doctor probed around in the flesh, cleaning the wounds. Nadja tried not to move or cry out, but the pain was tremendous. She lay back and stared up at the ceiling and prayed for the time to pass. Finally, after what seemed like hours but had been only minutes, the doctor complimented her on being so brave and left the nurse to bandage the wounds.

As she lay there, she looked down at her newly bandaged legs, and little red spots began to form—blood seeping through. She knew that the worst was over, but there was a long road ahead of her.

* * *

Nadja recovered from her wounds. It was a long slow process in which she needed to be given constant love and care, and had to "learn to crawl and walk for the second time" in her life.

Nadja remained living with her family from the start of the siege of Sarajevo on April 6, 1992, until August 28, 1995, when she was smuggled out of the city, first going through a tunnel and then by truck, under the ever-watchful eye of snipers. She traveled to the United States, where she began living with an American family that had agreed to care for her. She left behind her family, her country, her culture and the life she had known. She had lived through one of the longest military sieges in history.

Follow-up: Nadja

Nadja is now twenty-nine years old. She lives in Canada with her husband. She wrote a compelling book about her experiences called *My Childhood Under Fire* (Kids Can Press). Along with her writing, she is also a performer and public speaker, and she presents at schools for audiences of all ages about war—and more importantly—peace. She is a champion for the rights of children. She can be contacted to arrange visits at **mychildhoodunderfire@yahoo.com**.

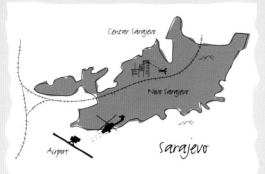

History of Bosnia-Herzegovina

The country of Bosnia-Herzegovina sits in close proximity to the centers of the large empires that have dominated Europe through the last twenty centuries. As such it has been under the domination of one empire or another for the course of almost its entire history.

The Roman Empire, centered in Italy, dominated the entire Mediterranean for hundreds of years, ending in approximately 400 AD. During the time of the Roman Empire, Christianity spread throughout much of the region, including Bosnia.

With the decline of the Roman Empire, another power emerged from the east—the Byzantine Empire—centered in Constantinople. This empire, which was dominant for close to one thousand years, also spread its religious belief system, Orthodox Christianity, which was in competition with the Catholic faith of Rome.

The Byzantine Empire started to falter, and there were competing powers, including Serbians, Croats, Hungarians and Venetians, all of whom, at different times, had influence in, or over, Bosnia. For brief times between these influences, Bosnia had varying levels of independence.

The periods of independence and domination by local powers ended in 1463, when the next great empire, the Ottoman Empire, expanded westward into Europe, defeated the Serbs and made Bosnia a Turkish province. With this conquest came yet another religious influence—the Muslim faith.

Ultimately the power of the Ottoman Empire declined, particularly in Europe, and in 1878 Bosnia-Herzegovina came under the control of the Austro-Hungarian Empire. This change again allowed greater European influence, as well as Christianity, to become more dominant. The resentment felt toward this domination came to a head with the assassination, in Sarajevo, of the heir to the throne of the empire. The entire continent was thrown into conflict, which became World War I. At the conclusion of the war and the defeat of the Austro-Hungarian Empire, there was another realignment of power.

A panoramic view of Sarajevo illustrating the vulnerability of the city to attack from the surrounding hills.

The Kingdom of the Serbs, Croats and Slovenes was created and Bosnia-Herzegovina became part of that monarchy. This country, whose name was changed to the Kingdom of Yugoslavia in 1929, remained independent until it was invaded and conquered by Nazi Germany during World War II.

1945—1981

At the conclusion of this war, and the defeat of Nazi Germany, all of Europe was reformed. During the reformation, the Kingdom of Yugoslavia came under the control of the leader of the resistance movement, Joseph Tito. Tito, whose father was Croatian and his mother Slovenian, brought together six republics, Serbia, Croatia, Bosnia-Herzegovina, Macedonia, Slovenia and Montenegro, and two provinces, Kosovo and Vojvodina, to form the Federal People's Republic of Yugoslavia. Under his iron rule, he was able to keep ethnic differences

67

and national sentiments in check and created a pan-Slavic country.

The conclusion of World War II was also the beginning of a further conflict, which was called the Cold War. This pitted the forces of Western Europe and capitalism and democracy, unofficially led by the United States, against Eastern Europe and communism, led by the Soviet Union. These two armed forces became NATO (North Atlantic Treaty Organization) and the Warsaw Pact, respectively. While the two forces never engaged in armed conflict, they engaged in an ideological war around the world. Although Yugoslavia was communist, Tito maintained independence from Soviet domination. He was able to maintain this country, while also limiting the outside influences of both Western Europe (democracy and capitalism) and Eastern Europe (communism). With his death in 1981, the country began to unravel.

1991–2007

The ethnic interests and national sentiments continued to rise within the different republics. With the end of the Cold War between the East and West, the desire for independence by the different republics, which had been escalating for the previous decade, came to a boil.

In 1991 two of the republics, Slovenia and Croatia, voted to leave Yugoslavia. There was opposition to the attempts of these two regions to leave the Federation. Slovenia was 90 percent Slovenian with the remaining 10 percent representing many other groups, including a small minority of Serbians, and the separation was accomplished with a minimum of violence.

This was not the case with Croatia, where there was more ethnic diversity, including 12 percent of the population being Serbian—the dominant ethnic group within the Federation. Croatia became involved in a substantial war, with the minority of Serbs within the Croatian Republic being supported by the armed forces of Yugoslavia, who were primarily Serbian. There was a war lasting over four years with minority Serbians either fleeing or being evicted by force from Croatia, and the Serbian army exercising its force and power in the ongoing war, trying to bring Croatia back into the Federation and drive Croats from territory they believed belonged to a greater Serbia.

In January, 1992, the Republic of Macedonia became the third republic to declare its independence from the Federation.

In April, 1992, a vote was held in Bosnia-Herzegovina to determine if they should become the fourth republic to leave the Federation. The members of the country who were Serbian boycotted the election, refusing to vote. Those who did participate in the referendum overwhelmingly voted to leave, and independence was declared.

Of all the republics of the Yugoslavian Federation, Bosnia-Herzegovina was the most ethnically and religiously diverse. While there are different accounts of the breakdown of the population, there was no group that formed a clear majority. Of the close to four million people in the newly declared country, 48 percent were Bosniaks, 37 percent Serbs and 14 percent Croats. These groups, for the most part, belonged to different religious groups, with the Serbs being Orthodox, the Croats Roman Catholic and the Bosniaks mainly Muslim. To further complicate the situation, these groups, which had previously lived in relative peace, were not limited to different geographic areas of the republic but were living side by side throughout the country.

Bosnia-Herzegovina had declared independence because it feared it would be dominated by the Serbs, who now formed a clear majority of the population, once the other republics declared independence. Those Serbian members of this newly declared country now feared that they would be dominated by the other groups who would be the majority of the population in Bosnia-Herzegovina. A war broke out which pitted the Serbs, supported by Yugoslavia, against the Croats, supported by Croatia and the Bosniaks. This conflict, which went from April, 1992, until the signing of the Dayton Peace Accord in November, 1995, effectively divided Bosnia-Herzegovina into two separate sub-states, one primarily composed of Serbs and the other Bosniaks. The conflict resulted in close to 100,000 deaths and 1.8 million people being displaced.

Sarajevo became the capital of one of the states, the Croat-Bosniak Federation. It is estimated that during the siege of Sarajevo at least 10,000 citizens, including 1,500 children, were killed, tens of thousands of others were wounded and hundreds of thousands of people were forced to flee their homes to take up a new life elsewhere.

Religion

The three primary religions in the region are Islam, Eastern Orthodox and Roman Catholic.

The Orthodox Church—It has over 200 million adherents and is the primary religion in many Eastern European countries, including

Bulgaria, Cyprus, Greece, Macedonia, Moldova, Montenegro and Serbia. It considers itself the original church of Christ and the one that most closely maintains the traditions and teachings of the early church.

The Roman Catholic Church— It is the largest of the Christian denominations with over one billion adherents throughout the world and is the dominant religion in many Western European countries, including Italy, France, Spain and Portugal. It is centered in the Vatican, in Italy, and is under the authority of the pope. It was created after differences with the Orthodox Church, and formally subdivided in the eleventh century. There was a further schism in the fifteenth century with the creation of the Protestant movement, which presently is the second largest Christian faith with 590 million adherents.

Islam—It is the second largest religion in the world with 1.4 billion adherents worldwide. It follows the teachings of the Qur'an, which was established by Muhammad in the seventh century. It has two main subgroups, the Sunni and Shi'a sects, which have divided into other groupings. Islam recognizes many of the prophets of the Bible, including Adam, Noah and Moses and believes that Jesus was a prophet, but that Muhammad was the final prophet.

Differences/Similarities

The similarities between the Orthodox Church and the Roman Catholic Church are much more significant than the differences. In fact, all Christian denominations, as well as Islam and Judaism, have common roots. All three religions share Abraham/Ibrahim as one of the most important prophets. However, despite their common threads, the three consider themselves to be inherently and fundamentally incompatible concerning their ideas about God and faith.

Clean the Field

Yugoslavia was an ethnically diverse country with no one group forming a clear majority of the population. Within the country, however, there were many places where one group did form a clear majority. When different regions of the country declared independence this decision was based on that region feeling that it was ethnically different from the country as a whole. Within these regions, there was most often one group that did, in fact, form a clear majority. The members of the minority groups often migrated to a place where they would no longer be the minority.

Some of this migration could be described as voluntary. Prior to the declaration of independence, or subsequently, these people decided they did not wish to be part of the newly created country or in a part of the country where they would be in a minority. It is important to note that even if the decision to move was "voluntary," it was often fueled by fear of persecution, violence or even death. People made a decision to move before they were forced to move— or were killed.

Unlike other regions that declared independence, Bosnia and Herzegovina had no clear ethnic majority: varioius ethnic groups lived in every region of the country. Close to half of the population of Bosnia, 1.8 million people in a total population of 3.9 million people, were displaced by the war.

At the time the conflict started in Sarajevo in 1991, the population was 50 percent Bosniaks, 34 percent Serbs and 7 percent Croats. In 1997 the population was 87 percent Bosniaks, 5 percent Serbs and 6 percent Croats.

The term "ethnic cleansing" has become synonymous with the conflict in Yugoslavia. Members of minority groups were beaten and had their homes, schools and churches/mosques attacked or destroyed. The "field was cleaned" of the minority group to allow the majority group to take over the land or to eliminate the possibility of support for the opposing armed forces. In the Bosnian conflict, there were regular forces made up of armies and militias and there were guerilla groups comprised of civilians. The Chinese revolutionary leader, Mao Zedong, stated that a guerilla fighter "must move among the people as a fish swims in the sea." Ethnic cleansing drained the sea, giving the fighter no place to hide.

When an individual is killed because of his or her ethnicity, it is called a hate crime. When large numbers of people are killed for this reason, it is called genocide. Genocide is defined by the United Nations as "acts committed with intent to destroy, in whole or in part, a national, ethnic, racial or religious group." It is a crime under international law. The United Nations determined that genocide did take place during the Bosnian conflict. While they did not assign blame to any one country, they have brought criminal charges against individual military leaders of the Serbian-supported armed forces and militia.

TOMA

How Could so Much be Lost so Quickly?

Toma helped her mother bring out the food for the midday lunch. As the oldest daughter in the home, at nine years of age, she was responsible for helping with the meals. They set down the bowls and the big pot on the table, which sat in the shade under the big tree in the courtyard of their compound.

Her mother, Arbaba, began filling the bowls with the sweet-smelling porridge, made with sorghum, onions, okra, all in a tomato sauce. Everything in the meal was grown on the land farmed by her father. Toma passed the bowls to her family who were already seated.

The first bowl, the biggest of course, went first to her father, Khamis. He was not only a successful farmer and the head of their family, but he was the chief of the village. He was the person to whom everyone came for advice, to solve disputes or, if an agreement could not be reached,

to finally make the decision that all would abide by. He was known as being fair and honorable, and he was, in some ways, like the father for the entire village.

Next Toma put bowls down for her brothers. First, came Sadam 11, then Amed 7, and Malik, who was 6. After serving the males, she served her sister, Sayeda, who was 8. Finally she placed a bowl before her mother's place and the last one for herself.

Toma was sad that they couldn't be at school today. They hadn't been to school for weeks. It wasn't close. They would leave at seven in the morning, taking some of the family's donkeys, and ride for two hours. Then, after being in school for four hours, they would ride back. It wasn't the distance that was stopping them now, though, it was the danger.

Armed men, roving gangs of militia, known as the Janjaweed, attacked members of the tribal groups. Villages were raided, burned to the

Toma, right, in Forbranga, a refugee camp on the border with Chad.

ground, people killed, kidnapped or raped. And it was rumored that these men were supported by the government soldiers who were supposed to be protecting the villagers.

For Toma these were all just stories. In her village all was quiet and calm and peaceful. It was as it always was. She couldn't imagine any of those things happening here. Her father wouldn't allow anything bad to happen.

With the meal finished, the girls began cleaning up and the boys began to hook up the water containers to three of the donkeys. They were going to bring water up to the house from one of the village wells. That's when they heard the sounds. It was faint at first, like a popping sound… then it got louder. It was gunfire.

They stopped and turned to stare at their father. He'd know what to do. He looked scared. Now Toma was scared.

"Everybody into the huts!" he yelled.

Toma froze in place, unable to comprehend what was going on, unable to move. "Everybody, hide in the huts!" her father yelled. Still she didn't move.

The sound of the gunfire got louder, and she could hear screams and the horses' hooves pounding against the ground, but still she couldn't move.

Toma was practically yanked off her feet as her mother grabbed her by the hand and pulled her and Sayeda into the girls' hut. Their father led the boys into the hut where the boys slept. They were two little structures, made of branches and straw, that sat on either side of a small building constructed of brick and stone where her parents slept.

As they scrambled into the hut, Toma looked back, trying to see over the fence that surrounded their whole compound. Straw and branches could keep the chickens in and wild animals out…but what good would it be against men on horses?

"Quickly, get under the mattresses, hide under the beds!" her mother yelled.

Both girls began crying, and their mother grabbed Sayeda and forced her to hide, piling the mattress and blankets and clothing on top of her until she had disappeared completely. Toma suddenly felt so exposed, so vulnerable, and she too scrambled under her bed. She felt her mother piling things on top of her.

"Both of you stop crying!" their mother yelled. "If they find you they will kill you!"

Hearing those words, the sobs got caught in her throat. She was terrified but knew she needed to be silent. She placed a hand against her mouth, trying to force the sound to stay inside of her.

The silence inside the hut only made the sounds outside even louder. There were tremendous shrieks and screaming, punctuated by rapid loud gunfire, all against the background of the horses' hooves, so loud that it was almost as if she could feel the earth trembling under her. She tried to picture the scene outside but knew she couldn't allow that. She closed her eyes tightly and covered her ears, blocking out the sound, trying to pretend that none of this was real, that none of this was happening… but she knew.

The adults of the village tried to keep things away from the children, but Toma was old enough to not only hear the hushed stories but to understand what was being said. Even worse, she had seen strangers passing through her village—people who had had their homes burned and their livestock taken. Just then she thought of the four family donkeys that were tied up just outside the gate. What was going to happen to the donkeys? No, forget the donkeys, what was going to happen to her family…what was going to happen to her?

She wasn't sure of the passage of time. It seemed like she lay there under the mattress for hours.

The sounds started to fade, and then there was silence. Finally she heard movement in the hut and was relieved to hear her father's voice, calling for them to come out. She pushed away the blankets and covers, and the mattress was lifted off of her.

"Are they gone?" she whispered to her father.

He nodded, and she felt an instant sense of relief.

"They are gone," he said. "For now."

Her sense of relief vanished, replaced by the fear she had just experienced.

Outside the hut, everything seemed the same. The sun was still shining brightly overhead and the bowls were still there on the table where they'd been left. There was no sight or sound of anything…there was no sound at all. It was just silent, as though even the wind had stopped blowing and was holding its breath, waiting, watching, wondering.

It was then that she noticed the smoke rising into the sky, thick and black. Her father had noticed as well. They followed behind him as he went through the gate of their fence. The donkeys that had been tied to the fence were gone. Looking beyond that she searched for the cattle that had been grazing. They were gone as well. Maybe they'd just been spooked and had run off. She could hope, but

REPUBLIC OF THE SUDAN

Population: 39,000,000

Location: Latitude: 15° N, Longitude: 30° E, Northern Africa

Area: 2,500,000 square kilometers

Climate: arid desert in north, tropical in south

Languages: Arabic (Official)
Nubian
Ta Bedowie
dialects of Nilotic

Ethnicity: Black 52%
Arab 39%
Beja 6%

Religions: Sunni Muslim 70%
Indigenous beliefs 25%
Christian 5%

Life Expectancy: 49 years

Infant Mortality Rate: 92 deaths per 1,000 live births

Per Capita Income: $2,400

Literacy Rate: 61% (male 71%, female 50%)

she knew that when the Janjaweed came they often took all of the livestock. She was grateful that the goats and sheep and chickens that were inside the fence were still safe, and she hoped that the animals at the farm would be all right.

They moved together toward the source of the smoke. It was coming from the far side of the village. Other people came out of their huts and as they walked their numbers increased until it seemed like everybody in the village was with them. There on the outskirts of the village were the charred remains of people's huts. Sitting on the ground were the women and children—people she had known her whole life—crying. The men poked through the ashes trying to find anything that had survived the flames. There was almost nothing, just like there was almost nothing that could be done to help.

The men gathered together and talked. Loud angry words were spoken, but she wasn't welcome to hear what they spoke about. Instead she stayed with the women as they made arrangements for the families that had been burned out to stay with other people. Whatever was lost was gone. What remained in the village would be shared with those who now had nothing.

The women talked as well, and Toma heard them speak. They said how terrible it had been—the huts burned and livestock taken—but they were grateful that nobody had been

killed and the Janjaweed were gone. Maybe they wouldn't return. *Maybe* seemed like such a small word. No protection from what might still happen. They were gone, but what was to stop them from coming back?

* * *

There was a pounding on the door of the hut and people were screaming! Toma and her sister jumped to their feet and ran out to the courtyard. Her mother and brothers were already there, but where was her father? Then she remembered…he'd already be at the farm. Outside the fence, people were running away, riding donkeys, trying desperately to drive cattle that didn't want to be driven.

Nobody needed to tell Toma what was happening. Her family ran through the gate and joined the people running from the village. As she ran she heard shots. She turned and looked over her shoulder, and her heart froze. Coming into the far side of the village were armed men on horses and camels. They were firing their guns and screaming. People were running in front of them, but they were no match for the racing horses and would be quickly overtaken!

The people in front of her ran off the path and scrambled into the tall grass, hiding from the pursuing men. Still holding her sister's hand, her mother holding the other, and her brothers in front of them, they all abandoned the path and followed behind, hoping to hide before the men reached them. Off the road they continued to run through the undergrowth, moving quickly, trying to stay silent. Finally the people in front stopped running, satisfied that they were far enough to be safe, not hearing any sounds pursuing them.

Toma lay in the grass, her heart pounding, straining to catch her breath again, while trying desperately to listen to any sounds in the distance. All was quiet.

"What are we going to do?" Toma asked.

"We'll wait a little longer and then go to the farm."

To the farm! To their father! He'd know what to do.

Toma's mother got the children to their feet. It was time to move.

The family farm was a small patch of fertile land, close to ground water. There they grew the vegetables and fruits that they either ate or traded to support the family. It wasn't far—they could only hope it was far enough that it hadn't been noticed by the armed men.

Some of the people from their village moved along with them. Others branched out heading to their own patches of land or to where they knew somebody was tending to a herd of grazing animals.

It wasn't long before they reached the farm and told their father what had happened. He hadn't heard any of the sounds, but by now the sky was filled with evidence of what was happening back in the village. They stood there together, watching as thick black smoke rose up into the air, marking the spot where the village was located. More homes were being burned.

"We have to hide," Toma's father said. "Everybody come."

He led them into the tall grass that lay on the one side of their farm, and once again they took refuge where they couldn't be seen.

After some time they heard a different noise, but it wasn't horses and it wasn't from the ground. It was the sound of a helicopter. They scanned the sky until they could see it—a big military helicopter off in the distance. For a fleeting second Toma thought that meant that the government had sent it, filled with soldiers to chase away the armed men—then she remembered what she had heard. The helicopters and the soldiers weren't there to stop anything. They were there to watch, sometimes even to help the armed men on horses. Even if there were soldiers, they weren't going to stop anything.

They stayed in the grass all day, eating some cucumbers and watermelons from the farm. The helicopter had long since gone, and the fires had stopped. The evidence, the black smoke, had been blown away by the winds.

Slowly, cautiously they moved back toward the village. As they walked they were joined by other members of their village. Larger numbers seemed safer, but really there was no safety. They just presented a bigger target.

Some of the men, including her father, went ahead. When it was deemed safe the women and children were called to follow.

Toma could not believe what she saw. The village was gone. All that remained of almost all of the buildings and fences were charred, still-smoldering remains. A few dead chickens and dogs that littered the ground were all that was left of the animals. The rest were gone, stolen.

People moved through the village, expressions of stunned disbelief on their faces. Hopelessly, desperately, men poked through the ashes trying to glean anything of value that might have survived the pillaging and the flames, but there seemed to be nothing. Possessions that couldn't be taken were scattered about the ground where the huts had stood.

How could so much be lost so quickly? What would drive these men to not just steal, but to destroy? Why did they hate them so much? Why couldn't anybody stop them? So many questions swirled through Toma's mind. And then she saw the bodies.

Lying on the ground, scattered through the smoldering remains were the bodies of people who had not been able to flee in time.

"Look away," her mother warned. "Don't look at the bodies."

Toma wanted to look away, but she couldn't. These weren't just strangers. These were friends, neighbors and even family members. Tentatively the survivors moved away, picking their way past the bodies. Some looked like they were just sleeping. Others, though, bore the evidence of what had killed them—crushed skulls, wounds and puddles of darkened, blood-stained dirt flowing out from beneath them.

They stopped in front of where their home used to be. The fence and the two huts were nothing more than smoldering embers. All that remained was the stone and brick building where her parents slept. Scattered about the property were a few items—a blanket, some clothing, cooking pots. Everything else was gone.

Toma's mother slumped to the ground against the tree. She buried her face in her hands and began to cry. At first it was soft, but then it became louder and louder until her whole body was convulsed in sobs. Toma tried to console her mother, and the children all gathered around trying to console her with their words and touches. Never had they seen their mother this way before.

Finally, their father appeared and spoke to her, stopping the tears.

"A decision has been reached," he said. "Tomorrow, before light comes we will leave."

Toma was shocked to hear these words. How could they leave their home, and where would they go?

"We should stay and fight," Saddam said.

"Fight with what?" their father questioned. "They have guns and we have nothing. They have taken our animals. They have destroyed our homes. When they come back, there will be nothing to take except our lives. We have to leave before they return."

"Maybe they won't return," Toma found herself pleading.

Her father placed a hand on her shoulder. "They will return. I must protect my family the best way I can. The men of the village have spoken. We've decided. Tomorrow we leave… all of us…the whole village."

Follow-up: Toma

Toma, her family and members of her village walked, mainly hiding during the day and moving at night. At one point during their journey, they were met by Sudanese soldiers. The soldiers beat her father and some other men, taking what little money they had, before allowing them to leave. It took five days of walking for the village group to reach a refugee camp on the border of Chad.

Now three years later they remain there, unable to return to their home due to ongoing dangers presented by the marauding militia. Toma's family, along with up to three million Sudanese, are alive due to the humanitarian relief efforts of international aid organizations, including the work of the United Nations. Toma's father, Khamis, as a respected elder, is responsible for helping to ensure that aid is distributed fairly in their camp.

Despite the massive effort, the aid has not been sufficient and tens of thousands continue to die from starvation, lack of medical attention and diseases caused by malnutrition.

Toma remains an ongoing victim of war.

SUDAN

Geography

Sudan is the largest country in Africa, about one-fourth of the size of the United States, and stretches from the sub-Sahara to tropical Africa. It shares borders with nine countries (Central African Republic, Chad, Democratic Republic of the Congo, Egypt, Eritrea, Ethiopia, Kenya, Libya and Uganda) and the Red Sea.

The Nile River and its tributaries cut through the length of the country. Despite the presence of these major tributaries, lack of water and drought are major issues throughout the country, particularly in the north, and less than 7 percent of the country is arable. This lack of water and arable land has often put different people in conflict over the scarce resources available for farming and grazing.

The capital, Khartoum, is situated at the conjunction of the White and Blue Nile rivers and is home to close to three million people. Literacy levels are low, especially for females, and health, education and social services are very limited. At times of drought, many people suffer from famine and are severely limited in their ability to feed themselves.

History

The land that now constitutes Sudan has been settled for over sixty thousand years. In ancient times it was known as Nubia. The Egyptian Dynasty dominated the Nile, and the northern parts of Sudan came under Egyptian control. Christian crusaders overwhelmed the area in the sixth century but were eventually replaced by Arabs, who spread the Islamic faith. In the sixteenth century, the Fung conquered the northern parts of Sudan while different African tribal groups came to dominate the south. In 1874 Sudan once again came under the control of its neighbor to the north, Egypt. This was short-lived, as it became part of the British Empire in 1898.

The British saw Sudan as being two very different regions and administered the north and south as two distinct entities—the north was Arabic and Muslim, and the south was African and Animist.

At the conclusion of WWI, there arose increased internal desires within these countries to seek independence, and the influence of the British Empire began to wane. The people of the Sudan continually pressed for independence. In 1956 the two regions, north and south, became the independent country of Sudan.

Recent History

Sudan has been politically unstable throughout its entire history, with numerous governments, political coups, military dictatorships and a lack of true representative government. It was often seen as a battleground in the Cold War between the Soviet Union and the United States. At times it was controlled by a Marxist government and has been seen as supporting international terrorism. It has been the target of Western or US economic sanctions and, in 1998, a cruise missile attack on a factory in the capital.

Partly because of and partly as a result of this lack of stability, Sudan has suffered through an almost continuous civil war throughout its time as an independent nation. There has been a constant conflict between the people and interests of the north and south of the country.

Prior to gaining independence, there was concern in the southern regions that they were going to be dominated by the north. Through political negotiations, and then violence, people in the south fought against being included as part of the larger nation and fought to have greater power and wealth. Civil war broke out, pitting the Muslim, Arabic-speaking northern region, against the southern region.

While there were times when the war was less intense and others when it was more lethal, it extended from one year before independence in 1955 and lasted until 1972. This left at least 1.5 million people killed and millions displaced both internally within the country and to countries surrounding Sudan.

This constant state of war left an already destitute country unable to harness its resources, either natural or human, as war destroys infrastructure and diverts money and attention away from caring for the people through education, health or general welfare, to security and weapons.

The civil war was finally ended when the Addis Ababa Peace Accord was signed in 1972. This allowed for the southern area to become a single administrative region with defined power and considerable autonomy in making many political decisions that related to their region. This agreement allowed the two regions

The cooking area in Toma's family's shelter in the Forbranga refugee camp. Up to three million Sudanese are displaced and living in camps, relying on international aid groups for humanitarian relief.

to coexist in relative harmony with no major civil unrest. However, there was always a sense of mistrust between the people in the two regions.

During the early 1980s it was felt that the central government, in the north, was attempting to undermine the autonomy of the southern region. There were attempts to replace local administration and to implement Islamic laws and the Arabic language in the south. This was in complete violation of the Peace Accord, and these efforts were met with protest—both peaceful and violent—in the southern region.

This conflict was also fueled by the discovery of deposits of oil in the southern area of the country, and disputes over how these resources would be exploited and how the revenue would be divided between the two regions.

The Sudan People's Liberation Army (SPLA) became the dominant rebel group to both protect the people of the south from the soldiers of the north and to advocate for the creation of greater independence and a change to a more democratic form of government. They launched attacks against government troops and facilities.

This second civil war—although some historians simply view it as an extension of the first since it was driven by basically the same unresolved issues—broke out in 1983. Once again people were killed, property, crops and infrastructure were destroyed, millions of people fled the fighting and the limited resources of the country were directed to war rather than the betterment of the people. If anything, this war was even more brutal and lethal than the first phase of the civil war. It is estimated that by the time the conflict ended in 2005, that almost two million civilians were killed and that over five million people were displaced, fleeing the war and its effects.

In January, 2005, a peace accord was signed that once again allowed the southern region considerable autonomy, a share of revenue from oil production and the right to peacefully form a separate country in six years if the majority of the people wished that end. In some ways this mirrored the previous agreement with the further condition being the consideration of total independence.

The Crisis in Darfur

In a country with limited resources, war and drought left it even more destitute. This became a crisis point in the western region of the country, known as Darfur, bordering the country of Chad. This conflict had been simmering for years with occasional flares of extreme violence.

The majority of people in the region are from three African tribal groups—the Fur, Masalit and Zaghawa. They tend to be mainly farmers living in small villages, defined by tribe and extended family. The Arab groups often survived by tending to migratory flocks. It is important to note that both groups are primarily Muslim, so religion was not seen as a source of conflict. Instead, in a country which experienced periods of drought, these two groups often came into conflict for scarce resources.

In 1998 a major episode of violence ensued in which over sixty Masalit villages and one Arab village were burned to the ground, and hundreds of people were killed. The government attempted to quell these disturbances, but there was always a feeling that there was a bias against the African tribal members and that the Arabic-speaking people were supported by the government. The African people did not believe that the government would support and protect them, or prosecute Arabs who were committing crimes against them. Two militia groups, the Sudan Liberation Army (SLA) and Justice and Equality Movement (JEM), acted to protect the interests of the tribal groups and to advocate for greater autonomy, or even independence, from Khartoum.

Outright conflict broke out in 2003. Government troops were sent in large numbers to the Darfur region. Roving gangs of militia, known as the Janjaweed, began attacking members of the tribal groups. These militias were supported and armed by the government. Villages were raided, burned to the ground, and people were killed, kidnapped or raped. These militia members were often accompanied by government soldiers or given air support (providing reconnaissance, dropping bombs or strafing civilians on the ground).

International attention became focused on this conflict. It was identified by outside sources as being genocide, and the United Nations Security Council passed a resolution demanding that the government intervene and control the militia. Basically the government denied all allegations against it, refused to restrain the militia and would not allow the intervention of United Nations troops to provide security and protection. The United Nations, often divided by the interests of member states, was not able to launch any sort of effective response to what was clearly seen as genocidal in nature.

Sudan did, however, originally allow a small number of troops from the African Union (AU) to be stationed in the country. These troops were poorly equipped, underfunded and undersupplied and were far too few in number to provide any form of security to the region. They were also given a mandate to only observe but not intervene or protect civilians. They could document massacres but not act to prevent them.

In addition, attempts to provide humanitarian aid—food, water and shelter—to the displaced people were thwarted by the ongoing danger and warfare in the country and efforts by the government to not allow them to intervene. Violence and threats of violence toward international aid workers caused great restrictions in the ability of these non-governmental organizations to provide aid. As with many conflicts, the death toll, especially for children and the elderly, was higher due to the effects of the conflict—disease, famine and lack of shelter—than from the actual violence of the conflict.

Hundreds of thousands of civilians fled Sudan during this conflict, moving into Chad. This has had a destabilizing effect on Chad—a country as poor as Sudan—which does not have the resources or wealth to easily absorb large numbers

Children, many orphaned and alone, remain victims of the ongoing crisis in the Sudan.

of refugees. The Chadian government also believed that the Sudan government was supporting and arming rebel groups within its country, as well as allowing the Janjaweed militia to cross the border and attack Chad villages, steal cattle and kill Chadian citizens.

Throughout the ongoing conflict, there were continual attempts by the United Nations to advocate for the disarmament of the militia, allow aid to displaced people and pursue a course of peace. The United Nations issued statements saying that there was a "scorched earth campaign" of ethnic cleansing, that it was the world's greatest humanitarian crisis and comparing it to the genocide in Rwanda.

In response, the Sudanese government consistently refused to acknowledge the extent of the crisis or its role in supporting the militia, or follow through on commitments to disarm them, or protect aid workers and supplies. Attempts to broker a cease-fire continually faltered. It was only in 2007, four years after the conflict reached a boiling point, that the Sudanese government agreed to allow a joint UN and African Union force to be deployed in its country. This will provide a more comprehensive peace-keeping mission and allow for better distribution of humanitarian aid to help those who have been displaced, their villages and livelihood destroyed. This effort continues to be thwarted by political interests.

It is estimated that well in excess of four hundred thousand people, mostly black Africans, were killed by the Janjaweed militia and the conditions they created, and over three million people have fled their homes to seek refuge from the killing. These people remain unable to return to their homes for fear that they will be killed or because they simply have no place to return to.

Animism

The term comes from the Latin word *anima*, which means breath or soul. It is considered the oldest of human religions. While many religions (Islam, Christianity, Judaism) believe that people possess a soul that transcends life, the Animism belief is that all objects contain a soul or spirit and that these spirits are continually interacting throughout the universe. It also differs from those religions in being a polytheism—a belief in thousands of Gods—as opposed to a belief in one supreme being or monotheism. In this regard, Animism is more closely linked to the Hindu faith. In Animism there is a highly interconnected relationship between people, other life forms, inanimate objects and naturally occurring phenomena, such as storms, fire or earthquakes. All these possess spirits and souls, and these can interact in a positive or negative manner with humans, depending upon the care, circumstances and ceremonies that take place. While it is ancient in origin, it is still practiced, in differing forms, by millions of people around the world.

Colonialism and its ongoing influence in Africa

Throughout the course of human history, different civilizations have become more dominant at different times. In the eighteenth century the European powers were dominant. They possessed weapons, transportation and technology that allowed them to exert their influence on places around the world. There was a great deal of competition between European powers to secure the resources of countries around the world. In Africa, virtually the entire continent was carved up by the European powers. The British Empire controlled almost one-third of the continent, and France, Belgium, Portugal, Spain, Germany and Italy all had extensive colonies.

The creation of these colonies often followed geographic features—rivers, mountains, lakes—but did not always take into account the culture or language of the people. Tribal groups could be divided among two or three countries, and some countries were created that contained tribal groups who were very different or even traditional enemies. In addition, there were often different roles and powers given to the various tribal groups which caused existing conflicts to become more deeply rooted and problematic.

With the collapse of these empires the colonies became independent countries based on the artificial borders created by the colonial powers. These divisions created tensions that have led to certain groups taking a dominant position at the expense of minority groups, or civil wars, or ongoing wars between different countries in attempts to gain power, people or land, or to offer protection to their tribal groups being persecuted in other countries.

The boundaries between countries are not always clearly defined, and in most cases almost impossible to defend or protect. People move freely over these borders, at times not even aware that they have crossed from one country to another. These borders are also not always recognized as legitimate, as allegiance to tribal members, who may live across a border, is seen as a stronger loyalty.

At times of conflict or crisis in one country, it is common for tens of thousands, or even hundreds of thousands, of refugees to seek shelter in a neighboring country. This influx of people creates political instability and taxes the very limited resources of the host country. There is virtually no country in Africa with the resources to adequately care for hundreds of thousands of refugees.

As noted, Sudan is an artificial grouping of two very distinct peoples which is a root cause of much of the civil unrest that has dominated the country's history. In addition, the boundaries between it and its neighbors are, in some instances, still the source of conflict and competition. The ongoing crises in Sudan have had a destabilizing effect on its neighbors, as refugees have fled to them, seeking protection and sustenance.

AFTERWORD

When *Elephants Fight* tells the stories of five childhood victims of war and conflict from around the world. There are countless other stories like these—many other children like Jimmy, Nadja, Farooq, Annu and Toma. This book hopes to give a face—if not a voice—to the suffering that is the result of adult conflicts. Children are unwilling participants in the violence that continues to rage in many places around the world, and only when adults take responsibility for their actions and recognize the incalculable cost of war on their children, can the grass be protected from the senseless violence and indiscriminate waste that is warfare and conflict.

Fifty percent of the royalties from this book will go directly to GuluWalk and will help the children of northern Uganda who continue to suffer the impacts of war.

For more information and to find out how to get involved visit **www.guluwalk.com.**

It is the energy and hope of the children that inspires the GuluWalk Foundation.

INDEX

Page numbers in **bold** refer to photographs and illustrations.